Praise for Kevin Tate's
Sustainable Software Development

S0-AEA-181

Rob Trubon
Mike McGlynn
Ryan Agee
Sue Lafortune

"Over the years I have seen the software development pendulum swing from one extreme to the other, as deficiencies in 'best practices' at one end of the spectrum spawned a new set of 'best practices' at the opposite end. Kevin Tate's book has finally brought the pendulum to a screeching halt, right about dead center. This book provides a balanced and practical guide to what's important if your goal is to develop software that lasts."

—Mary Poppendieck, Poppendieck.LLC.
Author of "Lean Software Development"

"1) In this very practical and accessible book interspersed with real-world examples and personal opinions, Kevin has distilled his years of developing quality software into a set of principles and practices that have been proven to work. If you are thinking of introducing an agile development environment (ADE) into your organization or of improving the one you already have, this book will help you clearly understand the benefits of a sustainable ADE, establish the practices to make it happen and coach you through the follow-up required to change the culture of your organization to make sure the changes take hold.

I am currently faced with exactly this challenge and this book has already given me several ideas I am looking forward to trying out.

2) In an industry plagued with missed deadlines despite long overtime hours, this book offers a refreshing alternative: a set of guiding principles and simple practices to follow that allow you to get the job done by working smarter, not harder. Drawing on the author's extensive experience developing quality software, the book clearly explains the principles behind a sustainable agile development environment, why it works, the practices to make it happen and the follow through required to turn these practices into habits."

—Peter Schoeler, Technical Director, Artificial Mind & Movement

"It's a familiar scene—the schedule's tight, people are putting in heroic efforts to get everything done, then at the last minute a change request comes in that wipes out the gains you had finally managed to make in meeting your ship date. Looks like it's pizza at your desk for the weekend again! An unfortunate situation to be in but a pattern that repeats itself all too often. "Sustainable Software Development" offers hope to break this cycle. It shows how a change in mindset can free you from the tyranny of unrealistic expectations and brings development realities out onto the table for everyone to see. By following these techniques you will be able to define and manage a software development environment that will work for the long haul."

—Kevin Picott

Sustainable
Software
Development

ESSEX

NORTHROP GRUMMAN

9020 Junction Drive, Annapolis Junction, MD 20701
301-617-8900

Essex Agile Library Book

Sustainable Software Development - Book #101

Please Return This Book to Our Library!

The Agile Software Development Series

Alistair Cockburn and Jim Highsmith, Series Editors

Agile software development centers on four values identified in the Agile Alliance's Manifesto:

- Individuals and interactions over processes and tools

- Working software over comprehensive documentation

- Customer collaboration over contract negotiation

- Responding to change over following a plan

The development of Agile software requires innovation and responsiveness, based on generating and sharing knowledge within a development team and with the customer. Agile software developers draw on the strengths of customers, users, and developers, finding just enough process to balance quality and agility.

The books in The Agile Software Development Series focus on sharing the experiences of such Agile developers. Individual books address individual techniques (such as Use Cases), group techniques (such as collaborative decision making), and proven solutions to different problems from a variety of organizational cultures. The result is a core of Agile best practices that will enrich your experience and improve your work.

Titles in the Series:

Alistair Cockburn, *Surviving Object-Oriented Projects,* ISBN 0-201-49834-0

Alistair Cockburn, *Writing Effective Use Cases,* ISBN 0-201-70225-8

Lars Mathiassen, Jan Pries-Heje, and Ojelanki Ngwenyama, *Improving Software Organizations: From Principles to Practice,* ISBN 0-201-75820-2

Alistair Cockburn, *Agile Software Development,* ISBN 0-201-69969-9

Jim Highsmith, *Agile Software Development Ecosystems,* ISBN 0-201-76043-6

Steve Adolph, Paul Bramble, Alistair Cockburn, and Andy Pols, *Patterns for Effective Use Cases,* ISBN 0-201-72184-8

Anne Mette Jonassen Hass, *Configuration Management Principles and Practice,* ISBN 0-321-11766-2

DSDM Consortium and Jennifer Stapleton, *DSDM, Second Edition: Business Focused Development,* ISBN 0-321-11224-5

Mary Poppendieck and Tom Poppendieck, *Lean Software Development: An Agile Toolkit,* ISBN 0-321-15078-3

Craig Larman, *Agile and Iterative Development: A Manager's Guide,* ISBN 0-131-11155-8

Jim Highsmith, *Agile Project Management: Creating Innovative Products,* ISBN 0-321-21977-5

For more information visit www.awprofessional.com/series/agile

Sustainable Software Development

An Agile Perspective

Kevin Tate

✦ Addison-Wesley

Upper Saddle River, NJ • Boston •
Indianapolis • San Francisco • New York • Toronto
Montreal • London • Munich • Paris • Madrid
Cape Town • Sydney • Tokyo • Singapore • Mexico City

The author and publisher have taken care in the preparation of this book, but make no expressed or implied warranty of any kind and assume no responsibility for errors or omissions. No liability is assumed for incidental or consequential damages in connection with or arising out of the use of the information or programs contained herein.

The publisher offers excellent discounts on this book when ordered in quantity for bulk purchases or special sales, which may include electronic versions and/or custom covers and content particular to your business, training goals, marketing focus, and branding interests. For more information, please contact:

U. S. Corporate and Government Sales
(800) 382-3419
corpsales@pearsontechgroup.com

For sales outside the U. S., please contact:

International Sales
international@pearsoned.com

Visit us on the Web: www.awprofessional.com

Library of Congress Cataloging-in-Publication Data:

Tate, Kevin
    Sustainable software development : and agile perspective / Kevin Tate.
      p.   cm.
    Includes bibliographical references.
    ISBN 0-321-28608-1
  1. Computer software—Development.   I. Title

QA76.76.D47T38 2005
005.1—dc22

2005019120

Copyright © 2006 Pearson Education, Inc.

All rights reserved. Printed in the United States of America. This publication is protected by copyright, and permission must be obtained from the publisher prior to any prohibited reproduction, storage in a retrieval system, or transmission in any form or by any means, electronic, mechanical, photocopying, recording, or likewise. For information regarding permissions, write to:

Pearson Education, Inc.
Rights and Contracts Department
One Lake Street
Upper Saddle River, NJ 07458
ISBN 0-321-28608-1
Text printed in the United States on recycled paper at R. R. Donnelley in Crawfordsville, Indiana
First printing, October, 2005

To my grandparents, Harris and Alberta Tate,
who were always there for me.

Contents

Acknowledgments

To say that I now have an appreciation for the amount of work that goes into writing a book is an understatement. People like Pierre Berton who can crank out enjoyable book after enjoyable book are a wonder, especially when they can still cling to a normal life that features a job, family, friends, and hobbies. I have a great job and work with fun and smart people and, it goes without saying, I treasure my family above all else, so I guess I neglected hobbies and keeping in touch with friends, so I am looking forward to getting back to a more normal lifestyle.

I couldn't have written this book without the support and patience of my wife, Claudia Morawetz, and my two kids, Andrea and Heidi. Their willingness to give me a few hours on weeknights and many weekends to work on this book are what made this project feasible. Special thanks are also due to Jim Highsmith. I had the pleasure to work with Jim intermittently through the last few years, and in many ways I credit Jim with the inspiration to write this book. Jim always provided timely and useful feedback and insights, and he was particularly good at helping me see the positive side of some of the negative reviews received as the book took shape.

There were many reviewers who contributed to this book. I've appreciated all the feedback, whether positive or negative. Kevin Picott, Tom Poppendieck, and Jim Markham in particular spent a great deal of time providing me with detailed, constructive input that was instrumental in clarifying the text and its presentation. Paul Petralia, the editor of this book, helped guide me through all the usual first-time author misunderstandings and problems, and Michelle Vincenti kept everything moving.

I'd also like to thank all my co-workers past and present. I've learned something from each of you. The NetWare connectivity team applied the principles of sustainable development which led to my rapid acceptance of agile development: Richard Sniderman, Martin Wolf, Larry Philps, Tom Kelly, Andrzej Szyszkowski, and Sam Vuong. Today, I'm still learning at Alias Systems and I'd like to thank David Wexler for giving me permission and support to write this book, and Peter Mehlstaeubler for sponsoring the introduction of agile development at Alias. I'd especially like to thank all the people who became actively involved as leaders in our change to an agile way of working: Mark Davies (who took the first plunge with his team), Milan Sreckovic, Kevin Picott, Ania Lipka, Lisa Fung, John Gross, Gerry Hawkins, Lynn Miller, Tom Wujec, John Schrag, Jey Michael, Theresa Edwards, Steven Watanabe, Ian Ameline, Thomas White, Paul Tokarchuk, Martin Watt, Chris Gailey, Moira Minoughan, Brian Kramer, Cory Mogk, Jim Craighead, Paul Breslin, Thomas Heermann, Al Lopez, Larry Philps, Christina Elder, Jerome Maillot, and many others.

I would also like to take this opportunity to thank the teachers who have influenced and inspired me. In high school, Mr. Ens (math) taught me what mental discipline was and Mr. Haight (history) was probably the best all-around teacher I've ever had. In university, Herb Yang, Jean-Paul Tremblay, and my thesis supervisor, Ze-Nian Li, were all influential.

I am glad this project is over and I promise my family and friends to not take on another big project—at least for a while!

About the Author

Kevin Tate is Chief Product Architect at Alias Systems Corp., a leading innovator in 3D computer graphics software, custom development, and training solutions for the film and video, games, web, interactive media, automotive, industrial design, education, and visualization markets. At Alias, his role encompasses development, methodology, product architecture, and technology strategy. He has more than 20 years' experience in the software development industry. Kevin is a dedicated cyclist, canoeist, and lover of the outdoors. He lives in Toronto, Canada with his wife and two children.

Foreword

Sustainable Software Development encompasses what I consider the two critical concepts in agile development—building adaptable teams and building adaptable products. Using these concepts enables teams to deliver value to their customers in the short term and sustain the capability to deliver additional value over time. You can have an incredibly talented agile team—put them to work on a clunky, poorly designed, ineffectively tested, spaghetti coded, legacy system—and it will not be able to deliver sustainable value to customers. Conversely, you can have a superb product in all those dimensions—and the wrong team can turn it into a poor, unsustainable product, very quickly. *Sustainable Development* helps us think clearly about the continuing delivery of customer value, from both a team and a product perspective—iteration by iteration, product release by product release.

Three themes dominate Kevin's book—sustainability, balance, and context. Sustainability means developing the capability to deliver customer value today and tomorrow. Agility is the art of balancing—short term versus long term, anticipation versus adaptation, ceremony versus informality. And finally, because every project team and every project is different, one must understand the specific context of each project in order to adapt practices to that context.

Sustainable development delivers value to the customer today *and* keeps the cost of change low in order to deliver value in the future. In agile circles sustainability has been applied to people, as in maintaining a sustainable pace of work. But products are also sustainable—or not. I remember a company whose product had an 18-month QA cycle—they reached that "unsustainable" position a little at a time, but the cumulative effect of neglect was non-responsiveness to their market.

Kevin identifies four principles of sustainability—working product, design emphasis, continual refinement, and defect prevention. In each of these areas he then aggregates a number of practices into a coherent whole. For example, the chapter on design provides a vision of design and then shows how a number of practices (not usually found aggregated together) contribute to that design vision. Practices in this chapter include guiding principles, design patterns, refactoring, simple design, reuse, re-architecture, and rapid design meetings.

Sustainability depends on the art of balancing. Agility can be defined as the art of balancing flexibility and structure, anticipation (planning) and adaptation. I use the term art because there is no silver bullet—no one answer. To illustrate this idea of balancing, Kevin uses a juggling analogy of keeping four balls in the air—the elements of continual refinement, working product, design emphasis, and defect prevention.

The journey from agile novice to agile artist requires first learning agile practices, and then learning how to adapt them and balance one with another. In Chapter 6, "Emphasis on Design," Kevin shows us how to balance the anticipation practices of guiding principles and design patterns with the adaptation practices of simple design and refactoring. If traditional methodologies can be accused of overemphasizing anticipation at the expense of adaptation, then agile methodologies can be accused of overemphasizing the reverse. Kevin's perspective helps practitioners find a middle ground—just enough, but not too much anticipation, combined with effective adaptation. Wouldn't it be wonderful if software development was simply one way or the other? But it's not. It's not simple. It requires artistic balance and Kevin gives us an insight into his own balancing artistry.

Finally, we need to understand the factors that help us make balancing decisions. These factors provide the context for making project decisions and adapting agile practices. In their book, *Shared Voyage: Learning and Unlearning from Remarkable Projects*, Alexander Laufer, Todd Post, and Edward Hoffman relate stories from several remarkable projects including the Advance Composition Explorer project at NASA and the Joint Air-to-Surface Standoff Missile project for the U.S. Air Force. This remarkably agile-like book shows how agile principles can be applied to aerospace projects. One of the three prime objectives of the study that resulted in this book was, "to enhance awareness to the different contexts surrounding different projects." How the NASA and Air Force teams applied practices and principles was context specific. Kevin provides us with key insights into adapting agile software development practices to specific situations, to specific contexts.

Kevin was practicing agile techniques before they acquired the *agile* moniker, and his lengthy experience in software product development shines through in this book. Aggregating practices into his four categories provides great benefit and the material is immeasurably strengthened by Kevin's real life, practical experiences that manifest themselves through his fascinating stories, tips, and examples.

I met Kevin about five years ago when he was instrumental in bringing agile practices to his company. It turned out to be one of my favorite agile enablement experiences, due in great measure to Kevin's leadership of the change process. Chapter 7, "Continual Refinement," delves into change practices from the perspective of a practitioner who has led the way.

There are two categories of authors in the agile movement. First, there are those like Kent Beck whose groundbreaking *Extreme Programming Explained* helped launch the movement into our everyday consciousness. Second, there are those like Mike Cohn whose wonderful book *User Stories Applied* extends our understanding of key principles and practices. Kevin's book lies in this second category—taking things we thought we knew and expanding them in new ways that make us think, "Wow, I wish I'd thought of that." To paraphrase Luke Hohmann (*Journey of the Software Professional*), enjoy your journey with a unique software professional.

Jim Highsmith
Flagstaff, Arizona
May 2005

Introduction

When I was a computer science undergrad in university, I received a coffee mug for Christmas. You may have seen this mug, it has a number of tongue-in-cheek expressions and quotes about software development and software programmers on it. Here's a random sampling:

> If a program is useless, it will have to be documented.
> If a program is useful, it will have to be changed.
> The value of a program is proportional to the weight of its output.
> Any program will expand to fill any available memory.
> Program complexity grows until it exceeds the capability of the programmer to maintain it.
> Hare's law of large programs: Inside every large program is a small program struggling to get out.
> A carelessly planned project takes three times longer to complete than expected; a carefully planned project will take only twice as long.

You get the idea . . . . My mug is copyright 1980 by Art 101 Ltd., and I find it interesting that most of the sayings on this mug have stood the test of time, apart from one that mentions "job control cards" and an antiquated list of programming languages such as JCL, Algol, and PL/1. However, one saying on this mug still stands out to me today:

> Weinberg's Law: If builders built buildings the way programmers wrote programs, then the first woodpecker that came along would destroy civilization.

I freely confess that this particular saying really gets my ire up. Perhaps I'm overly sensitized. I've had people quote it to me on a number of occasions; in particular, a former boss who felt that software developers lacked professionalism (he of course was a *professional engineer* and had the ring to prove it). Certainly what Weinberg says has a kernel of truth to it—that software developers can be a sloppy lot. But, by stating it as a law crafted as a negative statement, it implies that programmers can't write good software and don't pay attention to architecture, and that builders do. This is a slight to professional programmers, on the one hand, while being overly generous to builders on the other.

I am a big believer in the power of *metaphor*, especially in the context of technology. Sometimes, when faced with a highly technical term or feature to develop, it is incredibly valuable to use a metaphor that ties the term or feature into the real world through a simple comparison that everyone can understand. This is used in Extreme Programming, not to mention in many other technical fields such as usability analysis.

My real objection to Weinberg's Law is that it implies that a valid metaphor for software development is architectural engineering (i.e., building a building). It is astonishing how many people, from users to managers to software developers, believe this is a valid metaphor for software development when asked. Certainly, it is tempting to think that software is like building a building, and frankly what software developer, team leader, or manager wouldn't want to use the inspiration of Frank Lloyd Wright or the

Figure I-1
These buildings show different architectural styles and through their style and aesthetics also demonstrate the temptation to use buildings as a metaphor for software development. Left image ©Kathy McCallum, right image ©Steve Lovegrove. Images from BigStockPhoto.com.

Sears tower in Chicago as a metaphor for his or her work? Well-architected buildings are certainly interesting to look at, and exceptional buildings help define cities.

Why isn't building a building a valid metaphor for software development? The short answer to this question is that buildings are largely static and software is not. Buildings are very expensive to modify after they have been built, and indeed the entire process used to design and construct the building is intended to maximize the chances that the building will meet the customer's requirements and will, within some margin of error, stay within the desired budget. It's easy to identify when a building is complete, but successful software *never is*. Software is cheap to modify, and any successful piece of software is virtually guaranteed to change over its lifetime. Actually, the software industry has trained its users into believing that major modifications are possible, if not inevitable and expected.

Good software developers realize that their programs can be modified to add just about any unanticipated feature—of course, there are limits. Changing a web browser into a database or a scientific visualization application into a word processor might involve huge rewrites, but the key thing is that good software programs with good developers can do just about anything they want. "It's only software" is a common mantra.

Buildings, on the other hand, are another matter. Ask an architect to make an unanticipated change and chances are she'll reply that the only recourse is to tear the building down and start over. Ask an architect to design a building that will handle all the likely configurations and he'll refuse the project. This is because there are only a limited number of possible changes the architect and customers can make to the building over time. In software, unanticipated features are highly likely because software is developed in a highly complex, hard to understand, technical, and constantly evolving environment. After five years of use and modification, the source code for a successful software program is often completely unrecognizable from its original form, while a successful building after five years is virtually untouched.

These differences alone should be enough to convince you that software is not like "building a building" at all. And yet, the methodology taught in school to software developers, the methodology used in most software companies, and the methodology described in the bulk of today's software literature is exactly the same basic methodology, that is, used in building construction and other forms of engineering; the so-called "waterfall" method, which advocates thoroughly understanding user requirements before designing the software, followed by coding, and then testing.

I don't mean to imply that the waterfall method is plain wrong. Great works of engineering such as buildings, airplanes, bridges, and ships have been built with this method. And many of the practices introduced in the waterfall method are good. The problem as I see it is that too few people question the methods they are taught in school and the workplace. This is a human trait more than anything else and not a reflection on software developers in particular. It's just that probably the majority of projects would be better off using a more appropriate metaphor for software development.

If building a building is not a valid metaphor for software development, then what is? My favorite metaphor for software development is a coral reef. I think good software like Adobe's Photoshop, Oracle, SAP, Linux, and Microsoft Windows creates an entire *ecosystem* of customers, plug-in developers, distributors, VARs (Value Added Resellers), service and consulting firms, hardware manufacturers, and even competitors. This software ecosystem is like a coral reef.

A successful software product plays the role of the underlying coral in the reef. The coral is what makes the entire ecosystem possible. None of the other organisms can survive without it. And just like software, a coral reef is continually evolving, growing, and changing (though, of course, at a different pace!). It's not just the reef itself that is changing, it's the entire ecosystem with all its dependent fish, invertebrates (sponges, fans, etc.) that change and evolve together. The reef ecosystem is incredibly complex, yet also fragile and vulnerable, just as a software product's ecosystem is prone to disruptive technologies or competition. This level of complexity, growth, constant change, evolution, and vulnerability I believe accurately portrays the complex world that today's software products inhabit.

If you are a scuba diver, you should be able to appreciate this metaphor. Coral ecosystems are truly a wonder. You can view them from a distance or up close, noticing schools of fish, large fans, sponges, and hugely interesting and varied coral formations. And if you are fortunate to have visited the same reef over the course of a few years, you will also know how much a reef changes from year to year and season to season, despite the common misconception that coral is more like rock than a living organism. And the complexity of the ecosystem is obvious because it is impossible to understand the entire ecosystem at almost any scale, both when you can see the entire reef, and when you are watching only a small portion of it.

Figure I-2
Nature provides many useful metaphors for software and software architecture that accurately reflect the nature of software development. Successful software is like a coral reef because it inhabits a complex and continually evolving ecosystem of both complementary and competing technologies and software. Image ©Jason Sah. Image from BigStock-Photo.com.

Why does the metaphor we use to think about software development matter? Metaphors help us analyze a problem from a unique and common perspective. Good metaphors help groups of people grasp a complex concept or problem easily and clearly to understand what they are trying to build. In the software industry, we have been using the wrong metaphor, largely unconsciously, and have adopted practices from engineering that reinforce this metaphor.

Too many development teams develop software products as if they were building a building. They place too much emphasis on features of the building and trying to completely understand its requirements before it is built. The temptation is to finish the project or product and then to stand back and admire the creation. Inevitably, however, unanticipated changes come along in the form of user requests, bug fixes, and changes to other software or hardware that the program is dependent upon. The result is that over time, doors get added in odd places, walls get thinner and are moved around, cables get run through elevator shafts, and holes get added between floors or rooms. A mess accumulates that becomes increasingly hard to manage, and the greater the mess, the easier the temptation to add to it. Add in competitive pressures and a constantly changing ecosystem of underlying technology (operating systems, web browsers, databases, UI toolkits, etc.) and chaos ensues.

These projects are on the path to unsustainability. At some point the whole edifice will come tumbling down and become unmanageable. One of the main features will be an increasingly high cost of change where every change, no matter how minor, introduces a risk that something completely unrelated will break. The programmers will blame management, and management will blame everyone else. If the company can manage it, the application will be rewritten, only to start the clock ticking on the unsustainability cycle again. These projects aren't any fun, yet they are distressingly common in the software industry. The software industry is not slow-paced after all; laggards do not have high odds of survival.

This book, as you've gathered from the title, is about sustainable software development. The coral reef metaphor is an important one because the software industry needs to recognize that its principles and practices must support free-flowing, adaptive, and opportunistic evolution with the goal of surviving in the short term and thriving in the long term. Software projects are typically approached to meet one of short or long term, but not both. Either the project is a fragile edifice where the capability to meet customer needs over the long term is in doubt, or the project team spends endless analysis time that compromises its ability to ship, if indeed it ever happens. To deal with the short- versus long-term paradox, we need to *embrace* change, not be afraid of it, and we must recognize that software is complex, not pretend that it is simple. No software product stands completely on its own, and the development team must be able to interact with and foster its ecosystem. Good software products, companies, and the open source movement clearly exhibit these traits.

The principles and practices we use for project management, software architecture, and even those that help us effectively work together are hugely important in defining the richness of the ecosystem we want our product to inhabit and/or create. Linux, for example, would not be as successful as it is today if it weren't managed as an open source project, didn't have a modular architecture that allows multiple programmers to modify it at once, and have a license that allows businesses to freely use it.

Sustainable development is a pace that can be maintained indefinitely. This does not mean slower development—quite the opposite. Sustainability is not attained by artificially limiting work weeks to 40 hours as some books claim; the number of hours worked is an *outcome* of being in control of the project and having software with a consistently low cost of change.

Sustainable development requires a singular focus on a form of technical excellence that regularly provides useful software to customers while keeping the cost of change low. Achieving this is not easy because the more common forms of technical excellence concentrate on designing and writing *perfect* software while being change adverse.

This book describes the principles and practices required for change-embracing technical excellence; these principles and practices promote sustainability and result in faster development with less effort through having a consistently low cost of change. For teams who are used to unsustainable development, the experience is best characterized as liberating because they are able to deal with change, not be afraid of it or view it as a risk.

Sustainable development and technical excellence are vital parts of agile development. The agile development movement is challenging the traditional approaches to software development. As a result, I believe the software industry is on a path to creating a widely accepted new way to develop good software that uses the best practices from both traditional and agile practices. However, this is going to take time because agile development is so new and is only now starting to be noticeably employed in a widespread manner. It's going to take time for the mindset and practices to sink in to the industry, to be accepted, and to eventually be incorporated into the education given to new software developers. In short, I think the current debates in the software industry are healthy.

What I find particularly enlightening (and heartening) is that software developers aren't the only ones challenging the standard waterfall development practices. Huge and successful manufacturing companies are using lean manufacturing practices to get their products to market faster, and even traditional construction companies are beginning to embrace lean construction as a way to reduce costs and increase efficiency. Underlying all these new approaches, even though they are completely different industries, is the need to *connect* with customers to ensure that the resulting work meets the needs of customers, is built in the least possible amount of time with optimal efficiency, and essentially embraces the chaos of the short term to maximize the chances of long-term survival.

Balancing the short and long term requires projects to be more driven by a vision than tracked against a plan. Just as important, though harder to describe, is the conscious tradeoff being made in these approaches toward *good enough* analysis and documentation of the results of the analysis as opposed to an emphasis on the documents as the guarantor of success. By its nature, this relies on the people doing the work to be self-disciplined and professional as opposed to thinking that a process with its mandatory documentation applied to that group will provide the necessary results. This is a roundabout way of stating that agile development and lean methods emphasize flexibility and collaboration over stifling bureaucracy to minimize wasted effort. And this is why agile and lean practices are as much about culture change as they are about practices.

Where This Book Fits

I wanted to write this book because I see a need for it. Quite a bit of the agile development literature focuses on project management practices that promote agility. Project management practices are, of course, vital. But just as vital is the realization that in order to be agile, your software itself and the methods you use to develop it had better support your ability to be agile. You can't be agile if your software is brittle and is difficult to change with too few safeguards in place to enhance confidence in the changes. Software project management and development practices and software must go hand in hand.

I also feel that too many software projects focus exclusively on features and bug fixing and not enough on excellence. Software quality is an issue for our industry, but we too easily accept it as inevitable and somehow a result of the need for constant change. But as software becomes increasingly important in our daily lives, issues like security and quality are becoming more urgent. I think it's time we find ways to achieve features AND quality, not just view them as exclusive to each other.

As I see it, this book falls into a bit of an awkward spot. While this book is heavily influenced by the agile development community, and Extreme Programming (XP) in particular, agile in my opinion leaves too much to the imagination of the reader/listener, and this leads to many misconceptions. Some of these misconceptions are dangerous and very false—for example, that in XP there is no software design and that teams who practice agile development are somehow less disciplined. What I have tried to do in this book is expand on the existing agile literature by drawing on my work experience to introduce a team-oriented approach to achieving short-term and lasting excellence on a software project through principles (mindset) and practices.

I don't mean to imply that the outcomes, principles, and practices I describe in this book aren't employed at all in agile teams. I know they are, but sporadically and inconsistently. By not talking about these practices, it is too easy for traditionalists to dismiss agile development because it does not openly address some critical practices. The opposite is also true: Many of the practices in this book are advocated by the traditional software development community and are thus dismissed by some agilists. But I think this misses the point.

What I try to emphasize throughout this book is that what separates agile from non-agile practices is the *perspective* to the practice, not the practice itself. Hence this book's subtitle: *An Agile Perspective*. An agile perspective means in a nonbureaucratic way that emphasizes trying new things out and always learning, changing, and adapting as circumstances dictate—and with lots of collaboration. So maybe this book is a little bit like a bridge between the traditional and agile camps, but with an unerring bias toward agility. I hope that the saner minds in the agile community agree with me.

The Three Foundations of Agile Development

Agile development practices have three foundations: project management, technical excellence, and collaboration. Using the flywheel analogy from the excellent book *Good to Great* [Collins 2001], agility is just like trying to spin a massive flywheel. The forces that can be applied to the flywheel are the principles and practices you use for software development, which can be categorized by agile's three foundations as shown in Figure I-3. If any of your principles or practices are not agile, then this will act as a brake on the flywheel. That is, appropriate project management practices promote agility, as does an emphasis on collaboration within project teams and with customers, as does an emphasis on technical excellence, and all of these practices combined support agility. If a team employs agile project management practices but non-agile/inadequate technical excellence practices or little or no collaboration, the team's ability to be agile is going to be constrained.

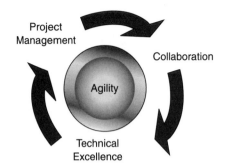

Figure I-3
The three foundations of agile development are the principles and practices used for project management, technical excellence, and collaboration. If agility is considered to be like attempting to spin a massive flywheel, then the principles and practices used for software development either act as a positive force or a brake on the flywheel. Hence, the principles and practices used for all three foundations must support and enhance each other.

About the Structure of This Book

What is needed for agility is a balanced blend of principles and practices that reinforce each other and the three foundations of agility shown in Figure I-3. The principles and mindset of sustainability are vital because they are the filter through which all the practices are chosen and implemented. Because of this, the core of the book (Chapters 4–7) consists of a chapter for each principle of sustainable software development, with practices that help implement the principle described in enough detail to get started. Chapters 1 and 2 describe sustainable and unsustainable software development, and Chapter 3 focuses on the important distinction between principles and practices. The closing chapter, Chapter 8, is targeted at creating culture change, because change is usually required to achieve a culture oriented around sustainability.

Quite a few of the practices described in this book are outlined in greater detail in other sources, and so I have included Appendix 4 with my recommendations for further reading. In general, when it comes to the foundations of agile development, project management and collaboration practices are typically described extremely well in the literature while technical excellence is often left as an exercise to the reader (except of course in Extreme Programming). Hence, I have tried to provide a slight bias toward the technical excellence practices.

I've consciously tried to ensure that this book is not just another technical book. I've encountered too many software developers who are brilliant architects and coders but don't, for example, understand the interdependence between their decisions and their company's larger business interests. I've seen too many projects that redesign their software simply for the sake of an elegant design when a pragmatic approach ("if it works, don't change it") is often in the better long-term interests of the project. I also have seen many teams who focus on creating the best possible software or, even worse, spending an endless amount of time writing requirements and design documents often with NO software and losing their focus on what every project's sole aim should be: shipping!

This book is for software developers, managers, and users who believe in self-discipline, professionalism, and in *shipping* software products with high quality that last. Especially for those who are looking for ways to embrace change and increase efficiency, while continually improving themselves, their teams, and their organizations.

Chapter 1
Sustainable Software Development

Sustainable software development is a mindset (principles) and an accompanying set of practices that enable a team to achieve and maintain an optimal development pace indefinitely. I feel that the need for sustainable development is an important but unrecognized issue facing software organizations[1] and teams today. One of the more interesting paradoxes in the high-tech sector is that while the pace of innovation is increasing, the expected lifetime of successful software applications is not decreasing, at least not in a related way. This chapter outlines the value of sustainable development, while the next chapter discusses the pitfalls of unsustainable development.

The more successful an application or tool is, the greater the demands placed on the development team to keep up the pace of innovation and feature development. Think of products like Adobe Photoshop, PowerPoint, SAP, or Oracle. These products are all successful and continue to be successful because their development teams have been able to meet user's needs over a long period of time despite persistent competitive pressures and changing technology and market conditions.

Unfortunately, there are too many projects where there is a myopic focus on the features in the next release, the next quarter, and the current issues such

---

1. My intended definition of *organization* is any group of people dedicated to a software project. Hence, it could be a software company, an IT organization, a software team, and an open source project. I assume that the organization is ideally multifunctional and so does not consist purely of software developers. Hence, the organization would include business people, documentation, usability and user interface designers, quality assurance, etc.

as defects and escalations reported by customers. The software is both brittle and fragile as a result of factors such as over- (or under-) design, a *code first then fix defects later* (*code-then-fix*) mentality, too many dependencies between code modules, the lack of safeguards such as automated tests, and supposedly temporary patches or workarounds that are never addressed. These are projects that are unknowingly practicing *unsustainable* development.

In unsustainable development, teams are primarily *reactive* to changes in their ecosystem. By and large, these teams are caught in a *vicious cycle* of reacting to events and working harder and longer hours akin to being on a treadmill or walking up a down escalator. The result is a project *death spiral*, where the rapidity of descent depends on the amount of complexity faced by the team and its principles and practices and discipline.

In *sustainable development*, teams are able to be *proactive* about changes in their ecosystem. Their ability to be proactive is enabled by their attention to doing the work that is of the highest value to customers with high quality and reliability and an eye toward continual improvement despite increasing complexity. These teams are in a *virtuous cycle*, where the more team is able to improve themselves and how they work together, the greater their ability to deal with increasing complexity and change.

Underlying sustainable development is a mindset that the team is in it for the long haul. The team adopts and fosters principles and practices that help them continually increase their efficiency, so that as the project gets larger and more complex and customer demands increase, the team can continue at the same pace while keeping quality high and sanity intact. They do this by continually minimizing complexity, revisiting their plans, and paying attention to the *health* of their software and its ability to support change.

Sustainable Development

Sustainable development is a mindset (principles) and an accompanying set of practices that enable a team to achieve and maintain an optimal development pace indefinitely. Note that optimal doesn't mean *fastest*—that would be pure coding, such as for a prototype.

Sustainable development is about efficiency and balancing the needs of the short and long term. It means doing just the right amount of work to

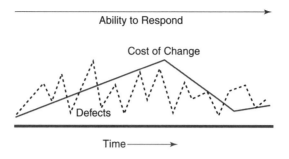

meet the needs of customers in the short term while using practices that support the needs of the long term. There are not enough software projects today where over time a team can stay the same size (or even shrink) and still deal with the increasing complexity of its software *and* its ecosystem *and* increasing customer demands. In sustainable development, the needs of the short term are met by regularly producing software that has the highest possible value to customers. This is done while keeping the cost of change as low as possible, which lays the foundation for future changes and makes it possible to quickly respond to changes in the ecosystem.

Sustainable development, as depicted in Figure 1-1, is a liberating experience for the lucky teams who can achieve it. While they have to deal with stress in the form of constant change, they have the advantage that they are *in control* of the situation and can outship their competitors because they are able to respond more rapidly and at a much lower cost. They are also able to be proactive about new technologies or new opportunities in any form.

Chemical Manufacturing and Sustainable Development

Some software companies are able to periodically reinvent themselves and their products. These companies don't need to completely rewrite their software products and in fact are able over time to add to their product line, usually with the same underlying technology and implementations. How do these companies do it? For some of the answers, let's look at some interesting research from a seemingly unrelated industry: chemical manufacturing.

Some interesting research into productivity at chemical manufacturing plants has parallels in software development [Repenning and Sterman 2001][2]. This research focused on chemical plants that are in deep trouble. These are plants that had low productivity, low employee morale, etc. The companies who owned the plants were seriously considering, or in the process of, closing them down and moving operations to another location with higher returns on investment.

What the researchers found is that in the plants in question the first response to trouble is to ask people to work harder, usually through longer hours. However, while working harder results in a definite short-term increase in overall capability, the long-term effect is actually *declining* capability, as shown in Figure 1-2.

One of the reasons for declining capability over the long term when working harder is the resulting vicious cycle or *death spiral*. This cycle is due to unanticipated side effects of the decision to work harder: As more hours are worked, more mistakes are made, and there is a greater emphasis on quick fixes and responding to problems. These mistakes and quick fixes lead to the requirement for more work.

In a chemical plant a mechanic might incorrectly install a seal on a pump. The seal might rupture hours or days later. When it does, the entire pump would need to be replaced, which takes an entire section of the plant offline while leaking more chemicals into the environment. People will think they aren't working hard enough, so they'll put in more hours. Then, the extra costs of all the overtime and environmental cleanups kick in and costs are cut in other areas such as carrying fewer spare parts to compensate. When parts aren't available when needed, the plant is down longer. The longer the plant is down, the greater the reduction in revenue and the higher the costs. The greater the reduction in revenue, the greater the pressures to further reduce costs. Eventually, people are going to be laid off, and the

---

2. In this section I decided to keep the author's terminology of *working smarter* and *working harder*. However, I do recognize that these terms are clichés, and it's not wise, for example, to tell someone he or she needs to work smarter or that the person is working too hard. Hence, in the remainder of this book I use working long hours and emphasizing feature development instead of working harder and continual improvement instead of working smarter. These are rough semantic equivalents.

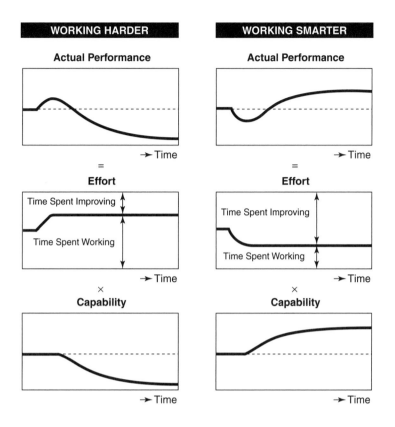

Figure 1-2
Working harder (more hours) results in declining capability over time. Working smarter, with an emphasis on continual improvement, leads to increasing capability. From [Repenning and Sterman 2001].

fewer people available, the less the ability of the plant to produce output. And so it goes.

Parking Lot Managers

I believe there are too many people in the software industry, managers especially, who judge the morale or productivity of their company by how many hours their employees work on evenings and weekends on a regular basis. I call these people *parking lot managers* because they're often *proud* of the fact that their company's parking lot is still full at midnight and on weekends. However, very few of these managers realize that full parking lot effort is not sustainable, that working harder may be valid in the short-term when a concerted effort is required, but it is definitely not in the best long-term interests of the company.

> Companies need people who treasure the contribution they make when at work and who are passionate about the success of the company. This has no correlation with the number of hours worked . . .

The largest reason for a decline in long-term capability is that working harder results in an inability to implement necessary improvements. In the plants studied, mechanics were too busy fixing problems in the pumps to do anything else. As any car owner who ignores basic regular maintenance knows, the longer mechanical parts are left untended, the greater the chance they will eventually fail, not to mention the greater the eventual cost. This leads to another vicious cycle: The harder people work and the more problems they are trying to fix (or more appropriately, the more fires they're trying to put out), the greater the chance that problems will continue to build and grow worse over time. No doubt you've been in situations like this. The problem quickly becomes one of having time stand still through continuous death march releases, or fixing things.

The employees of the chemical plants turned things around by developing a realistic simulation of their situation. The simulation was developed in such a way that it demonstrated to participants the results of various decisions. Importantly, the simulation was *not* designed to teach or test skills. They recognized that the mechanics, for example, didn't need to be taught to be better mechanics; after all, they were very adept at their craft through all the crucial problems they had to fix on the spot. The simulation, implemented as a game, realistically demonstrated the various important tradeoffs that can be made in a plant between working harder and *working smarter*. In a chemical plant, working smarter consists of activities like preventive maintenance, where a pump is taken offline, disassembled, examined, and lubricated on a regularly scheduled basis. Working smarter is also taking the time to examine the entire plant's systems and processes and continually attempting to identify problems before they occur while reducing the complexity of the overall system in order to increase efficiency.

The results of the simulation were an eye opener for the plant's employees. The results were also counterintuitive to many: They showed that working smarter (especially doing preventive maintenance) consistently produced better results over the long term. The simulation also demonstrated that with any attempt to work smarter there is an initial dip in capability caused by the need to let some problems go unfixed while initial improvements are made as shown in Figure 1-2. This helped the employees expect the dip in capability and have the persistence to follow through with the changes (a perfectly human response would be to think that the dip was permanent and revert back to the old ways). Eventually, as the number of improvements started to make a difference, capability would climb until a point where the plant entered a *virtuous cycle*, where each additional investment in improvements led to further efficiencies and gains in output with lower environmental impact, which in turn led to more time being available to make further improvements, and so on. People were actually able to accomplish *more* work by working smarter than they had before.

As a result of the simulation, the chemical plants described experienced a complete turn-around. Not only were these plants kept open, but they also received additional work and their business grew. And some of the changes introduced by the employees had a lasting effect, some with a return on investment of 700,000 percent! The most astonishing thing, which perhaps isn't so astonishing when you consider the rut these companies were stuck in, is that virtually all of the changes that were required to make the turn-around were well known to the employees but they'd never been implemented because they were always too busy!

Continual Improvement: The Accelerator Button

The study on capability in a chemical manufacturing plant is surprisingly relevant for software companies. The main lesson is that in sustainable software development, you need to strive for continual improvement while resisting the temptation to focus on features and simply working long hours to meet demands. A software company's business is only as sound as its factory, where the factory is made up of a number of "pumps"; the *software* that the company produces. You may need to take some of your pumps offline occasionally, and every few years you will realize that your factory is completely different than it was previously because of all the changes made to the pumps. And as with real-world factories, only in extreme circumstances, such as when a disruptive technology is on the verge of widespread adoption or a paradigm shift is about to occur, will you need to completely replace the factory.

Each of the following questions examines some of the parallels between chemical manufacturing plants and software development.

How many developers view writing test code, building testability into their code, enhancing a test framework, or cleaning up their product's build system as nonessential to their work and hence something that lower paid people should be doing?

Somehow, many developers have a mindset that non-feature work is not part of their job. This is not only preposterous but also extremely dangerous and is akin to a mechanic at a chemical plant believing the basic upkeep of his tools and workshop is not part of his job. If developers don't write automated tests, then chances are the culture of the company is focused on defect *detection*, not defect *prevention*. As shown in Chapter 5, this is the worst possible situation a software company can get itself into because it is extremely expensive and wasteful, with many defects being found by customers (which is the most expensive scenario of all). Likewise, if developers don't personally pay attention to the infrastructural details of their products (such as build and configuration management systems), it is all too easy for problems to creep in that eventually impact key performance indicators that also impact developer's productivity. Examples are build times, code bloat, source tree organization, and improper dependencies between build units creeping into the product.

How many managers refer to non-feature work as a *tax* that is unessential to product development?

If a company is in a feature war with its competition, the company's management needs to understand how the decisions and statements they make ultimately impact the long-term success of the company. Managers must recognize that they have a key role in leading the attitude of the organization. In this case, management, or even in many cases software developers themselves, need to realize that the only tax on the organization is their attitude about non-feature work. As in chemical manufacturing plants, it is counterintuitive that ongoing investment in continual improvement will lead to greater capability than solely concentrating on features and bug fixing.

How many teams are too busy to implement any improvements, such as adding to their automated tests, improving their build environment, installing a configuration management system, rewriting a particularly buggy or hard to maintain piece of code, because they're "too busy" developing features and bug fixing?

Just as the mechanics in the chemical engineering plants are unable to perform preventive maintenance by taking a pump offline on a regularly scheduled basis because they're too busy fixing problems (i.e., fighting fires), many software teams are also unable to pay attention to the "health" of the underlying software or the development infrastructure. As described earlier in this chapter, this is a key part of the software development death spiral. It will eventually lead to a virtual crisis with a team spending an increasing amount of time during each release fixing defects at the expense of other work. Either the company will eventually give up on the product or be forced into a likely rewrite of major portions of the software (or even the complete software) at great business expense.

When developers are fixing defects or adding new features, how often do they use shortcuts that compromise the underlying architecture because they're "under a tight deadline"?

The main danger with these shortcuts is that they're almost always commented (e.g., ugly hack introduced before shipping version 2) but rarely fixed. These shortcuts are *broken windows* (see chapter 4 for more details) in the software and are another part of the software death spiral.

Are the people who develop the products in your company proud of the products, but not proud of how the products were created?

If your products are absolutely brilliant but your people are burned out by the experience of individual releases, maybe it's time for a step back. Maybe there is too much heroism required, or too little planning takes place, or there is an ongoing requirement for long hours because the schedule is slipping. There are many possible factors, but the underlying cause can usually be traced back to a lack of focus on continual improvement and technical excellence.

The Genius of the AND versus the Tyranny of the OR

One way to think about continual improvement is through the genius of the AND and the tyranny of the OR [Collins and Porras 2002]. Software organizations need to stop thinking about features and bug fixing as being exclusive from underlying software health and infrastructure improvements. This is the tyranny of the OR; thinking you get features OR software health. By focusing on continual improvement through paying constant attention to sustainable practices, software companies will be able to achieve the genius of the AND: features and bug fixing AND underlying software health. Greater capability leads to an *increased* ability to introduce *more features* with *fewer defects*, and hence have *more* time to innovate, not less. Hence, focusing on continual improvement is not a tax it's an ***accelerator button***[3]!

A Sustainable Development Experience

I have been fortunate to work on at least one team that achieved sustainable development. In one case, I worked on a software project that was released to customers over the course of several years. Over this time, the capabilities, complexity, and size of our product increased but the number of defects in the product stayed constant and our ability to innovate *increased*. And our team did not increase in size. How did we do it?

- Our software worked every day.
- We relied heavily on automated testing to catch problems while we were working on new features.
- We had high standards of testing and code quality, and we held each other to those standards.

---

3. Jim Highsmith deserves the credit for this observation.

- We didn't overdesign our work and built only what our customers needed.
- We were uncompromising with defects, and made sure that all the known defects that were important to our customers were fixed in a feature before we moved on to the next one. Hence, we never had a defect backlog.
- We replanned our work as often as we could.
- We were always looking for ways to improve how we worked and our software.

Other teams in our company were incredulous that we could produce the amount of work we did *and* keep quality so high. For example, the company had an advanced practice of frequent integration, which was vital because the product was developed across many time zones. Because of our stability and quality we were able to pick up and fix integration problems extremely early in a development cycle. This was vital to the success of the company's products.

Think of Cobol when you think of sustainable development: The original developers of the Cobol language could not conceive of programs written in Cobol that would still be in use in 1999, and yet when the year 2000 came along, all of a sudden there was a huge demand to fix all the Cobol applications. Here's a related joke:

It is the year 2000 and a Cobol programmer has just finished verifying that the Y2K fixes he has made to a computer system critical to the U.S. government are correct. The president is so grateful that he tells the programmer that he can have anything he wants. After thinking about it for a while, the programmer replies that he would like to be frozen and reawakened at some point in the future so he can experience the future of mankind. His wish is granted.

Many years pass. When the programmer is woken up, people shake his hand and slap him on the back. He is led on a long parade, with people cheering him as he goes to a huge mansion. The master of the universe greets him enthusiastically. Pleased but puzzled, the programmer asks the master of the universe why he has received such a warm reception. The master of the universe replies "Well, it's the year 2999 and you have Cobol on your resume!"

Summary

Developing software is a complex undertaking that is performed in an environment of constant change and uncertainty. In the Introduction, I likened this to a coral reef, not only because of the complexity of the software ecosystem and the need for constant change, but also because of the fragility of existence. It is very hard to build or inhabit a software ecosystem that thrives over the long term.

Very little software is written once, installed, and then never changed over the course of its lifetime. And yet, the most prevalent development practices used in the industry treat change as an afterthought. Competition, the changing ecosystem, and the fact that users (and society in general) are becoming increasingly reliant on software, ensure that the software must change and evolve over time. The resulting combination of increasing complexity, need for change, and desire to control costs is a volatile one because very few software organizations and teams are equipped with the mindset, discipline, and practices to both manage and respond to complexity and change.

The answer to all the stresses placed on software organizations and teams lies in sustainable development, which is the ability to maintain an optimal pace of development indefinitely. In sustainable development, teams are able to be proactive about changes in their ecosystem. Their ability to be proactive is enabled by their attention to doing the work that is of the highest value to customers with high quality and reliability and an eye toward continual improvement *despite* increasing complexity. These teams are in a virtuous cycle, where the more the team is able to improve themselves and how they work together, the greater their ability to deal with increasing complexity and change.

The next chapter describes unsustainable development and its causes. This is important to understand before considering how to achieve sustainability.

Chapter 2

Unsustainable Software Development and its Causes

Unsustainable development, as depicted in Figure 2-1, is an all-too common situation today in the software industry. Most software teams place too much of a short-term emphasis on feature development and fixing defects and do not pay enough attention to the health of the underlying software. The result is software with a high cost of change, that is increasingly unmaintainable, and where every change has the risk of destabilizing the product.

In unsustainable development, teams tend to spend an ever-increasing amount of time fixing defects and stabilizing the software. Features still get developed, but less time is available for feature development due to the amount of time required to stabilize the software, which increases with each new release. This results in teams tending to become change-adverse while they are stabilizing the product because each change increases the risk that something will break. Teams tend to desire freezing of requirements as early as possible so they can get some work completed. This reduces their ability to respond to customer requests and changes to underlying hardware or software because they are spending too much time on stabilization, which is wasted effort, and not enough on new work.

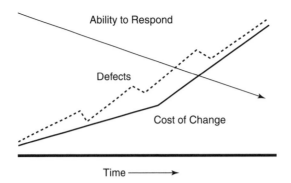

Figure 2-1
Unsustainable development is characterized by a constantly increasing cost of change to the software. The usual evidence of a high cost of change is a constantly increasing number of defects. Each change adds complexity and uncovers or causes defects that require more changes, and this complexity leads to a declining ability to respond to customer requests and changes to the ecosystem.

The symptoms of a short-term outlook are only evident once a threshold has been crossed. This is the point where the development team starts to spend so much time trying to keep up with the defect backlog that they are noticeably unable to spend enough time to develop new features. It may take only a few months or many years to reach this point. Many development teams may not even be aware how bad things are: Release cycles might become *death marches*, customers, management, and sales force complaints might get louder, and developers themselves will start blaming the problems on management ("if only they had listened to me...") and other developers ("they produce too much buggy code..."). It may take a while, but morale will eventually suffer then plummet; in extreme cases, people will lose their jobs through being fired, layoffs, or outsourcing, and customers will lose patience with the product and company.

Luckily, the extreme is seldom reached. Unluckily, most project teams live in a gray area that is not sustainable development but is uncomfortably close to unsustainability. These projects have not reached the threshold where the problem is obvious; developers feel like they are barely keeping up or are making slow progress but with too much stress. This is the software development *death spiral*, where the only variable between unsustainable projects is the rapidity of the descent toward obvious unsustainability.

Unsustainable Development and the Boiled Frog

If you are working on a project on the unsustainable development path, you may not be aware of it. Think of a frog and a pot of water. If you drop a frog into a pot of boiling water, it will immediately jump out. But if you put a frog into a pot of cold water and then slowly heat it up, the frog will stay put until it is boiled.

Have you ever been away from a project for an extended period or joined a new company and felt like you jumped into a pot of boiling water? It's amazing what we will tolerate if we've been in a situation long enough.

The difference between you and a frog is that you aren't a victim of circumstance. You have a significant ability to influence the temperature of the water through your actions and by collaborating with others. You can't directly control the temperature, but you can keep it within a comfort zone. But you have to be able to make an honest assessment of your situation and be willing to make changes . . .

Technical Debt and the Flywheel

The underlying cause of the inability to develop new features due to a defect burden is what is best called *technical debt*. Technical debt is caused by an accumulation of poor decisions over time—decisions that often seem right at the time but are usually made in the interests of a short-term quick fix to the software. Very rarely is it possible to identify a single decision that stands out as one where the problems might have started.

Jim Collins describes a relevant flywheel metaphor [Collins 2001]. Collins uses the flywheel metaphor to describe how decisions affect momentum in an organization. Think of a massive flywheel that is so large all you can do at first is give it tiny nudges that move it an inch at a time. Your organization's sustainable development emphasis is like continually providing tiny nudges. Each new nudge adds momentum to the flywheel so that it continues to pick up speed. However, every decision to develop a new feature or fix a bug by introducing an ugly hack or ignoring the underlying architecture acts as a brake on the flywheel. The software development death spiral results because these brakes, or nudges in the wrong direction, will eventually stop or even get the flywheel spinning backwards. How fast the flywheel is spinning and its direction is something your organization should be aware of.

The Perils of Jumping in Place

One strong piece of evidence for technical debt in the software industry is the number of products that must be completely rebuilt in order to keep up with competitive products or to respond to a major technology change. Completely rewriting a product requires a massive investment in effort and time, and the result is most often a loss of market share while the next generation (replacement) product is built. These companies are building new products to *jump in place*, to address the same market with a similar product! Even if the product is truly better, the loss of market share and customer mindshare is not easily overcome, especially since existing competitors will have gotten stronger and new competitors entered the market during the time required to build the next generation product.

An extreme example of losing market share when jumping in place is best dubbed the *Osborne effect* after Osborne Computer, Inc. Osborne produced one of the first portable computers in the 1980s. It was the size of a small suitcase and could barely fit under an airplane seat, yet it revolutionized personal computers at the time because it came preinstalled with useful software and was portable to some degree, something that is taken for granted today, largely thanks to Osborne. Not many users took advantage of the portability of the computers due to their size and weight, but it didn't matter because of the value of the system and its preinstalled software. Osborne had a successful computer on the market that was selling well. Then, for some reason, it decided to build a replacement rather than refining its current product. Osborne compounded its mistake by preannouncing the next generation of its computer with a larger screen, faster processor, etc. This was a huge mistake; customers stopped buying Osborne computers to wait for the new generation, cash got tight, the new product fell behind schedule, and soon Osborne Computer was in Chapter 11 bankruptcy.

Bankruptcy is the extreme end of a spectrum of lost market share. Lost market share in any form requires effort to get back to the former position, and this is wasted effort that technology companies must be diligent to avoid.

The Causes of Unsustainable Development

Why is unsustainable development so common in the software industry? It's because software development is a complex undertaking. Figure 2-2 depicts some of the factors that contribute to the complexity. There are a number of *project stresses,* which you can't control, that are trying to push your project toward unsustainability. Your only defense is to employ a number of things that you can control, or at least influence, to counteract the stresses and keep the project on a sustainable path. Get one or more of these wrong and your project is going to start into the death spiral. The project stresses are going to be different for every project, and over time the stresses are bound to change. Therefore, constant diligence is required on your part to keep the balance.

Project Stresses

User Requirements

User requirements continually evolve and change. It is virtually impossible to predict what users are going to require more than some small number of weeks to months in the future.

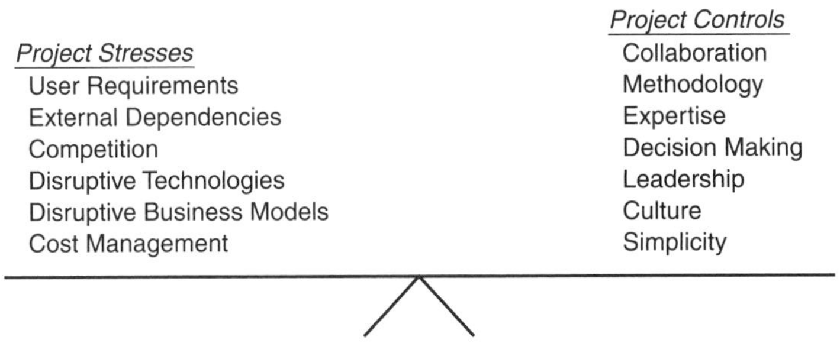

Figure 2-2
Software projects are subjected to a number of project stresses that can't be controlled. These stresses are a constantly changing set of forces that push your project towards unsustainability. You can employ a number of defenses that you can control or influence to try and keep the project on a sustainable path.

Project Stresses
- User Requirements
- External Dependencies
- Competition
- Disruptive Technologies
- Disruptive Business Models
- Cost Management

Project Controls
- Collaboration
- Methodology
- Expertise
- Decision Making
- Leadership
- Culture
- Simplicity

External Dependencies

Today's software depends on operating systems, libraries, third-party components, etc. Software usually also depends on computer hardware or hardware interfaces (especially if it's embedded). The steady advance of technology means that changes to these *interfaces* are a given. Managing these changes is a challenge and requires constant diligence and foresight. A change to any of these might set a software team back for days, weeks, or months as the new version of the operating system, compiler, device driver, libraries, web browser component, etc. is integrated and tested. And for many software teams, especially where it is impossible to dictate the end user's computing environment, the team must support the old *and* the new interfaces. This adds to development complexity and to the risk that the software will break in unexpected ways.

Competition

It is relatively easy to set up a software organization today because the barriers to entry are low. All that is needed are some bright people, a few computers, and a connection to the Internet to get started.

Unfortunately, what many companies lack is a workable business plan. They do not have a clear idea of their true market worth because they overestimate or do not know their market size, and they almost always suffer from an inability to adequately sell and market their work. They may be good at getting initial funding and making some initial sales, but most software organizations struggle to stay in business. Their very existence and sometimes more innovative products make it difficult for other companies to thrive.

Disruptive Technologies

The constant advance of technology means there is a need for continual innovation, or at least a need to keep up. Given that products need to meet users' demands over the long term, it is tempting to think that in every case it makes perfect sense to always do only what your customer wants you to do. In many cases, however, this may actually be a long-term recipe for disaster. Because of the constant advance of technology, it is possible for *disruptive* technologies and associated ways of doing business to eliminate established businesses, businesses that in most cases have done an excellent job of listening to their customers! [Christensen 2003] [Christensen and Raynor 2003] The problem is that most customers are not visionaries and are restricted by their current problems. Hence, they are really good at asking for 10% more than what they currently have, but if another solution, usually built on newer technology, comes along that offers them 50% more in one increment, chances are they'll take it.

Disruptive technologies usually start out looking like a toy to established businesses and their customers. Because they do not appear to be a threat at first or require a new way of doing business, the established businesses will ignore them right up until the time when their customers realize the advantages of the new offerings and decide to change. By then, of course, it's too late for the established business.

The Internet is an example of a disruptive technology. The Internet is a godsend in terms of providing a ubiquitous communication medium. Software and related services such as support and consulting can cheaply and easily be offered over the Internet. All businesses today must learn how to wisely use the Internet. They must also learn how to deal with the threats of the Internet, because it also provides an easily accessible means for hackers to exploit an internal network, for illicit software and serial numbers to be distributed, and also a forum for malicious people to exploit security flaws in software and distribute those exploits to unsuspecting users.

Disruptive Business Models

Equally disruptive to most organizations is a disruptive business model. Dell Computers is an example of this type of disruption. Dell does not innovate technologically; their innovation is the ability to produce computers on demand by clustering their suppliers together and taking all orders over the Internet. This gives them the ability to compete on price and responsiveness. Established PC manufacturers such as HP, Compaq, and IBM have not been able to keep pace or duplicate Dell's business.

Another example of a disruptive business model is open source software. The open source community is dedicated to producing software for free. Although virtually all of this software is only usable by highly technical people (typically other programmers) today, there is no question that open source will play an increasingly disruptive role in the software industry as usability plays an increasingly important role in open source projects. Microsoft has a well-established monopoly on the desktop market that is now being eroded in some sectors, such as in governments, because Microsoft cannot compete against free software. However, what remains to be seen with open source projects such as Linux is if the business model is sustainable, whether the open source community can keep itself going almost exclusively through support and services as claimed.

I believe it is important for all software developers and organizations to embrace open source. As I will argue later in this book, it is important that the software community stop repeatedly implementing commodity software components so that everyone can concentrate on their unique value. Open source is an ideal mechanism to make this happen. In addition, I believe the tools used for software development have not kept pace with the demands of modern software development. Many organizations and teams put a great deal of effort into building their own infrastructure (custom-built tools, bug tracking, and configuration management systems, etc.) when this type of infrastructure should be shared.

Cost Management

Organizations need to carefully manage how much they spend on software projects. Because of the complexity of software development, it is hard to control costs through greater efficiency. Achieving high efficiency is difficult because of factors such as the mindset of the organization, its processes, training (which does not emphasize efficiency), deadlines, etc. Hence, the easiest way to reduce costs is to employ cheaper people. This explains the increasing use of outsourcing of software development to countries such as India and China where labor is cheaper. But outsourcing is the easy way out. More people in the industry need to recognize the need for efficiency, because efficiency is at the heart of sustainable development.

Project Controls

Collaboration

Working effectively with other people in your organization and your customers is a crucial aspect of software development. If people are off doing their own thing, then the project as a whole suffers. Good things happen when people can cooperatively work together toward a common objective.

Methodology

The development methodology, the principles (mindset) and practices (project planning, design, testing, coding, etc.) you use, has a dramatic impact on the success of a project. Methodology directly influences efficiency, change tolerance, responsiveness, and software quality.

As described in the Introduction, an important factor is that we use the wrong metaphor for software development (that software development is like building a building). Because the metaphor is incorrect, teams either approach software development using plan-driven development, because that is what is taught to them in school as the approach used by engineers, or,if that doesn't work, they use variants of an ad-hoc *code-then-fix* approach.

Software teams who approach software development with little or no discipline commonly employ *code-then-fix*. Sometimes this is a reaction to practices that do not work for their project, and sometimes it is a lack of focus on technical excellence. These teams spend most of their time writing software and very little time on planning and analysis. Software developed this way is fragile and brittle and will resist change because even if good coding practices are followed, the lack of a set of sound practices will lead to a great deal of dead code and thrashing.

Plan-driven development is derived from engineering as it is applied to the design and construction of bridges and buildings. It is best typified by the ISO-9000 set of standards. The plan-driven approach is what is taught in schools to software developers because there is the mistaken belief that all the complexities in software and the target ecosystem can be understood before any code is written. This is rarely true over the short term and definitely false over the longer term.

Much of the emphasis in plan-driven development is on producing documentation of requirements, designs, test plans, etc. While documentation has value as an important means of communication, the main point is missed: that the real value comes from the *process* you have to go through to produce the documentation, *not* from the documentation itself. That is, having to work through a design with your peers is a valuable exercise because it fosters collaboration, understanding, and creativity; producing the document that describes the results of the discussion is less valuable, and the actual document is of even lower value because it must be maintained. By stressing the need to create documentation, plan-driven approaches achieve a mixed result, where on the positive side, stressing documents means that analysis work is required, but the result is too often that the effort spent producing and maintaining the documents detracts from the amount of time spent on analysis. Also, the emphasis on documentation has led many people to believe that the existence of the documents equates with discipline, when in fact discipline should be viewed as ensuring that the analysis work happens in the most efficient manner possible.

Plan-driven development also does not work for software development because it is impossible to put together a plan when the project starts that take into account all the changes in requirements and in the ecosystem that will occur over the course of the project. Also, plan-driven approaches stifle agility because they emphasize ceremony and documentation over having a working product in the erroneous belief that somehow having a pile of documentation describing requirements and design is proof that the project cannot fail, that a disciplined approach is being used, and that by extension any project that does not have this depth of documentation is not disciplined. The problem is that the effort put into the ceremony and documentation is wasted effort; many projects only wind up producing documentation when what they really needed was to get a working product into their user's hands and get feedback from them since that is the only way to really know if the desired system meets user needs.

Expertise

Expertise with software development and with the project's ecosystem is a strong indicator of success. Expertise allows teams to apply an increasing amount of intuition and to be able to understand what is important and what is not.

Decision Making

Your ability to make decisions in a complex and constantly evolving ecosystem, often with incomplete information, is crucial to success. An important aspect of decision making is *prioritization*, where you choose what must be worked on and when.

Leadership

Leadership helps set and communicate a vision, strategy, and tactics. Leadership helps to keep projects on track.

Culture

The culture of an organization shapes the attitudes and priorities of the people who work in it. Culture defines the requirements for leaders, how decision making is performed (and by whom), and the methodology. If a new methodology or leadership or decision-making style is required, then the culture must change.

Simplicity and Reliability

The vast majority of software today is overly complex, hard to use and learn, and has too many features for most of its users. Even commonplace applications like word processors are packed with features that most users never use. For example, one study showed that although the Office97 version of Microsoft Word had 265 functions, only 12 functions were used by more than 75% of users, and 42 were not used at all! [McGrenere 2000]

There have not been enough studies done to prove any ill effects of unnecessary complexity on users. However, I believe this is a significant issue as computing struggles to become more widely adopted, not to mention provide the productivity gains that should come through automation. Complexity is behind at least part of the outsourcing trend because one way to manage complexity is to get someone else to do it for you. Complexity is also why my wife asked me to return a recent Christmas present: I bought some software that claims to help process and manage digital pictures, yet after one look, she said the new software undeniably had some useful features but overall it would mean she would spend *more* time processing pictures than before.

When it comes to computing and simplicity, there is a huge disparity between what consumers want and what companies would like to sell them [Economist 2004]. Too many software organizations still compete on features and price alone. Unfortunately, they are often encouraged to do so by the most technical users, who are the early adopters of any technology, and by the media, who still publish reviews that contain feature comparison charts.

Related to simplicity is the need for reliability. Software is notoriously unreliable. Many users refuse to buy the first version of any software product, and users are frequently frustrated by version upgrades that break or remove features they relied upon in the previous version. Too many software organizations emphasize features over reliability.

There is not enough emphasis placed on simplicity and reliability. And yet, all one needs to do is look at Apple's iPod or a Palm PDA. These are simple and reliable devices that are popular because they do a few things very well. What is impressive about them is that a great deal of restraint was shown in their development. It's easy to add features but very hard to show restraint to keep them out. Is there a future where this type of thinking is applied to software?

Summary

Unsustainable development is a development pace that is typified by stress, frustration, and a sense of not being in control. It is most evidenced by a continually increasing cost of change and defect rate and a corresponding decreasing ability to respond to changing conditions. Unfortunately, unsustainable development encompasses a large gray area of declining capability with a variable pace of decline. As a consequence, unsustainable development may not be immediately evident, even to the people on the project.

Unsustainable development results from a complex ecosystem of continual change and stresses that are largely out of the control of an organization. Therefore, in order to achieve sustainability, the organization must recognize its stresses and continually adjust its defenses and coping mechanisms.

The next chapter returns to the theme of sustainability. It starts by describing the difference between principles and practices and then outlines some of the key principles that lead to sustainability. These principles are used to frame the practices described in the rest of the book, because sustainable development begins with principles (mindset) and uses practices that reinforce them.

Chapter 3

The Principles of Sustainable Software Development

In the traditional software organization, the emphasis in software development is on features, bug fixing, and *the plan*. Development proceeds in a linear fashion, beginning with analysis and design, the development of a plan, coding, testing, fixing of problems, careful tracking against the plan, and then use by customers.

This linear (waterfall) approach to software development is still the primary method of software development taught in schools. But this is an *engineering* approach to software development that isn't suited to software development as described in the Introduction.

At least part of the reason software firms are rarely able to achieve sustainability is because software developers do not receive an education that prepares them for the real world. In the real world of software development, software must be developed in a complex and changing ecosystem of technology, competitors, and customers. And it isn't until programmers are first exposed to the commercial world that the size of the code base they work on and the size of the teams they work in become significant. This is also the first time programmers have to write code and *live with it* for any meaningful length of time. Not just their code either—with personnel turnover there comes an increasingly large body of code that nobody on the current team wrote.

It's unrealistic to expect the education system to duplicate real-world conditions. This is because the education system needs to teach students their *craft*, which must be taught in a controlled environment so students aren't overwhelmed. But knowing a craft is only one part of what is needed. In order to provide a *bridge* from the academic to the practical worlds, we need a *mindset* that can be used to create a *culture* of software development. This should be the culture of *sustainable development* so that teams can achieve and sustain a high pace of development over the long term, despite all the surrounding complexity, without heroics. Otherwise, it's too easy to burn out on the profession.

Without the right mindset and culture, too many people try and fail with the methods they are taught. They then fall back on ad-hoc variants of the traditional linear approaches because the linearity provides a degree of comfort that progress is being made while also being familiar. But by being ad-hoc, there is either going to be too little structure (which is *code-then-fix* development) or too much, which applies too much bureaucracy in an attempt to keep the process under control. And bureaucracy tends to stifle innovation, flexibility, and change tolerance—the very properties that a dynamic and changing environment requires.

The bulk of this book, and most books on software development, are filled with practices and rules. Practices are too often treated as templates for success, when the reality is that practices must be tuned to the situation and team. And rules are a result of bureaucracy that is put in place to try to make software development more predictable. Predictability is often achieved, but at the cost of innovation and the ability to respond to customer requests. If your team implements a given set of practices but doesn't have the right mindset or culture that supports the practices, you're not going to get far. You will be better off than doing purely ad-hoc software development, where you will be *good* but not *great*.

Before your team talks about development practices you need to first focus on the principles you are going to follow. These principles should guide you every day in making tradeoffs and in fostering the right mindset and culture for your team and organization. The practices will follow from the principles you choose to adopt.

Why Principles Are More Important Than Practices

The difference between principles and practices is analogous to the difference between vision and features in a project. Unsuccessful projects start by defining a set of features that when put together are surmised to meet some user need. These projects are technology looking for a market, and the odds of their success are low. Successful projects, on the other hand, start with a clear user need and a vision of how to meet that need. The vision is simple and can be used to develop an initial set of features and a prototype that can be put in front of customers for feedback. The feedback is used to refine the feature set, which is then put in front of customers for more feedback, and so on. This is iterative development, as it is called in agile software development. The following are key aspects in the vision-oriented approach to product development:

- A user need and vision so it is clear what is being built
- Rapid refinement to adapt to change
- A close relationship with users so they can provide timely feedback
- Continual learning to refine the product so it best meets user needs while avoiding unnecessary features

Too many people are looking for a magic set of rules or list of practices that define the silver bullet of software development. Our education and upbringing reinforce this desire by using rules and step-by-step procedures to help us solve problems. We run into trouble, however, because we rarely recognize the role of complexity in the application of rules. Rules work best when the problem is simple but break down as complexity increases. But software development, and product development in general, is not simple.

In sustainable software development, the principles are like vision and the practices are like features. Principles define *what* you want to accomplish and the practices *how* you want to go about it. Too much of the mantra in software development is around sets of practices. We hear "follow this set of practices" or "if you aren't following these practices, you aren't using this technique." If only it were that simple! These practice-oriented approaches put the cart before the horse by defining the features before the vision. While there is no doubt that in every case the practices are valuable and can be learned from, if you don't know what you are trying to achieve, then your efforts are going to be misdirected.

The problem with practices and rules in the face of complexity, as in software development, is that it is too easy (and human) to lose sight of where you are going and what you want to accomplish, get bogged down in the details, and flail around. The most common response to flailing around is to apply bureaucracy, to define a set of strict rules and milestones that cannot be deviated from. But bureaucracy stifles innovation and is most often misguided, leading to unintended side effects. It is also inflexible and change-intolerant.

Some practice-oriented approaches provide a simple set of practices that are intended to lead to sustainable development. But, by stating their approach as a set of hard-and-fast rules, they mislead people into believing they are complete, when in fact they are not. Good teams apply these practices and can achieve success, but the chance of failure is still high because of the complexities inherent in software development and the people who develop it. Also, by stating that the practices must be adhered to, a different sort of bureaucracy or elitism develops where people say silly things like: "I won't work more than 40 hours this week because that is one of our practices," even though there is a critical deadline in the near future, or "We never design aspects of our architecture because we only design what we need today," even though it is plainly obvious that a bit of extra work today would make tomorrow's work, that everyone recognizes needs to be done, an order of magnitude easier.

Great teams recognize that *what* they are trying to achieve is more important than *how* they achieve it. They listen to the practices that are proposed to them, ask questions to understand what they are trying to accomplish, and then apply them as needed. Great teams see through the strict rule-based façade and are successful because they see rules as a solid foundation to build on. They work from a clear user need (high user value through features and high quality) and a vision (the principles) and continually learn and refine their approach (the practices) as their project progresses. This is what underlies sustainable development. To summarize, there are three elements to sustainable development:

- A vision and set of guiding principles[1] that define what needs to be accomplished.
- *Practices that are consistent with the principles.* The practices outlined in this book are not a set of rules. Instead, they are intended as building blocks that your team *should* refine and add to over time through continual improvement of your approach to software development.
- *A tight feedback loop of experimentation, learning, and refinement so that during the development of the project the project team is able to change, modify, and enhance their practices as required so the team can best fulfill the principles (vision).*

Applying the Principles of Sustainable Development

Given a vision and desire to achieve sustainable software development, the following principles apply:

- **Continual refinement** of the product and project practices.
- A working product at all times.
- A continual investment in and emphasis on design.
- Valuing **defect prevention** over defect detection.

Each of these seemingly arbitrary principles contributes to sustainability. Since the rest of this book outlines practices that support these principles, let's examine each principle in turn.

Continual Refinement of the Product and Project Practices

Continual refinement is a recurring theme in sustainable development. Software is complex and must evolve continuously over a long period of time in the face of changing user requirements and an evolving ecosystem

---

1. See Chapter 6 for a description of guiding principles.

of markets, partners, technologies, and competition. At the start of any project it is impossible to plan for all the required changes. Therefore, teams must plan for change and implement practices that enhance their ability to change. These practices must cover how they manage their projects, how they design their products, and also the practices used to develop the products themselves. To accommodate these changes, teams need user involvement and an emphasis on reflection, learning, and experimentation but also lightweight practices to keep themselves on track and monitor progress and risks.

Continual refinement is required for sustainable development because it defines a set of practices that establish a *heartbeat* for a project. This heartbeat establishes a steady rhythm that is used to keep the project going and continually monitor progress in a lightweight way.

A Working Product at All Times

A software product should always be in a working state. This doesn't mean it is always functionally complete, just that it works and has high quality. The longer the product is not working, the greater the chance that quality is degrading every working minute, and the greater the cost to get the software working again before completing the project. The goal of software teams is to ship their products, and by keeping a product in a state as close as possible to being shippable, the easier it will be to ship.

A secondary meaning to this principle is that the emphasis of the team is on producing a working product and shipping it, not on producing documentation of user requirements, software designs, etc. that *might* lead to a product. This is a key principle of agile development: The best way to get user feedback is to give users something they can really comment on, a product that is written to fit their needs even if it is only work in progress. Documentation, even if carefully reviewed, does not elicit the same quality of feedback as something that users can actually use. Even prototypes are better than a document.

A working product is required for sustainable development because it ensures that time is spent on productive activities. Effort spent getting the product back to a working state is wasted effort and a missed opportunity to be doing valuable work.

A Continual Emphasis on Design

Design is a key differentiator between products. Both good design and bad design are immediately obvious and can heavily influence purchasing decisions, but the most important aspect of design quality in terms of sustainable development is on the productivity of the development team. Design decisions and changes are made every day and by every member of the team, and the team needs to allow itself to make design changes *as appropriate* throughout the project. Traditional software development emphasizes trying to design the software to anticipate every possible future use at the beginning of the project or prior to the writing of any code. This does not work. Agile software development advocates designing only what you need today while not making silly decisions that close the door on future enhancements. Contrary to what some people believe, agile development actually requires a lot of design, perhaps even more than traditional approaches.

A continual emphasis on design is required for sustainable development because good design and sustainable design practices extend the life of the product by keeping the implementation in a healthy state that enhances maintainability and changeability while ensuring there is a simple long-term design vision.

Valuing Defect Prevention over Defect Detection

Defect *detection* involves trying to find and fix defects after changes have been merged into the production software. Defect *prevention,* on the other hand, emphasizes catching defects *before* the changes are merged into the production software.

The key symptoms of a defect detection culture are an undue reliance on defect tracking systems, manual testing efforts, and large numbers of defects that reach customers.

In the typical defect detection organization, organizations invest a great deal in a QA or testing organization. They have elaborate defect tracking systems in which members of the organization spend countless hours sorting, prioritizing, and assigning defects for fixing. And yet regressions (defects fixed or features introduced in previous versions of the product which no longer work) are still introduced in new product versions as features are added and bug fixes are made. The quality onus is primarily on QA and testers, and in many organizations a virtual wall is constructed between developers and QA. Developers produce new versions of the software, and then throw it over the wall to QA, who test it and then accept or reject it. The software may take weeks or months in QA before the product is ready to ship to customers.

In a defect prevention culture, defect-tracking systems are still required, but their importance is greatly reduced. This is due to much lower defect counts because development teams have multiple safeguards in place to ensure that regressions are never (or rarely) introduced in already existing functionality and that new features and bug fixes are properly tested and have safeguards that ensure they will not break in the future. A heavy emphasis is placed on automated testing so that people (QA and testers) can focus on testing the product in a realistic manner, in ways that mirror what actual customers will do with the product. There are no virtual walls in a defect prevention culture because ideally the testers are part of the team, and the quality onus is spread evenly between the developers and QA and testers.

An emphasis on defect prevention is required for sustainable development to ensure the development team is highly efficient and is putting its effort into creating value for the customer, not on wasted effort. Also, by minimizing the number of defects that reach customers, development teams are able to have productive conversations with users about features and workflow because users are able to use the product in realistic ways.

Striving for Sustainable Development Is Like Juggling

I like to use the metaphor of juggling when explaining sustainable software development. Striving for sustainable development is like juggling the six balls shown in Figure 3-1. Think of the entire team juggling together, like many minds controlling one pair of arms and hands.

The four small balls, each representing an element of sustainability, have a subtly different color, texture, and weight. If you drop one ball, you're still juggling but your outcome isn't going to be as good as it could be, and your audience (the customer) is definitely going to notice the mistake. Juggling demands you understand each ball, its

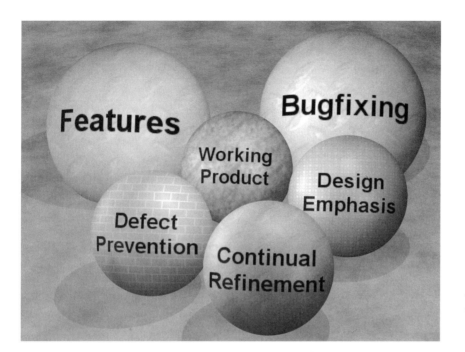

Figure 3-1
Software develop-
ment is like juggling
the four balls of sus-
tainable development
at the same time as
the much larger balls
that represent fea-
tures and bugfixing.
Instead of just jug-
gling the two large
balls, sustainable
software development
recognizes the genius
of the AND and
results in the ability to
juggle all six balls at
the same time, even
though they are dif-
ferent sizes and
weights.

shape, weight, color, and texture, and that you are able to focus on any one ball while keeping all four in focus.

The larger balls that represent features and bugfixing are completely different in shape and weight from the small balls. The complexity of the task of juggling the four small balls and two large balls usually leads teams to juggle only a few balls because that's much easier.

The team may juggle just the large balls. This leads either to the purely ad-hoc *code-then-fix* approach to software development or bureaucracy, consisting of milestones, rules, and mandatory documents. Unfortunately, these approaches ultimately lead to unsustainable development.

Or the team might juggle one or more of the small balls so they don't have to deal with the large balls. They'll produce awesome designs or have a working product or continually refactor their code, but they won't get anything done. And if they manage to ship and have customers, chances are the customers won't be satisfied.

Great software teams are able to juggle all six balls. They understand that juggling the small balls comes first because they are more predictable, and this makes the task of juggling the large balls much easier. This ability to accomplish the *genius of the AND* in the face of the *tyranny of the OR* leads to sustainable development while capturing the complexities required to do so.

Culture, by Descriptive Words and Phrases

Sustainable software development requires a certain kind of culture. While it is hard to completely describe the desired culture, it is possible to help focus on what that culture is by using some descriptive words and phrases.

Disciplined

The team must be highly disciplined in its approach and goal focused. Discipline is what the team uses to ensure that all the work is done properly and with no shortcuts. For example, discipline helps teams ensure that their work is *really* done when they say it is.

Unfortunately, agile development has been labeled as being undisciplined by some. Yet any team, regardless of its practices, will not succeed unless it is disciplined. What I suspect is happening is that there is confusion about the difference between discipline and *ceremony*. Ceremony in this case refers to the required activities that must be performed in a project: for example, a requirements document before a certain milestone, milestones such as a feature freeze, weekly status meetings, design documents, or mandated beta programs. Agile teams minimize ceremony in favor of keeping to the task at hand and producing results (a working product), while more involved processes emphasize ceremony and documentation over the results. In many cases, unfortunately, people mistakenly believe that unless documents are created there is no discipline. This is a mistaken belief however, because these documents are frequently wasted effort and are no guarantee that a prescribed process is being followed.

Responsible

The team must be responsible for its work and not play the part of a victim. Victims go along with anything and don't rock the boat, then absolve themselves of any responsibility so they can lay the blame elsewhere. There are actually very few situations in life where you are truly a victim. In most cases, the victim is just as susceptible to his or her own line of thinking and unwillingness to take charge of the situation as they are to the situation. For example, if a decision is made that a responsible person knows is wrong, that person doesn't just go along with it, he or she ensures that everyone is aware of the consequences so that the decision is either made with the right data or is changed. Victims, on the other hand, go along with the decision and then say, "I was told to…," even though they knew it was the wrong thing.

Responsible people have courage to take on any situation and do not get swept up by events. They trust others to do the best they can and are always diligent to ensure that nothing falls between the cracks. They don't just say, "that can't be done." They explain why and then help uncover the real problem and provide a viable alternative.

Leadership

The team has multiple leaders who work together, and the leaders are not just the managers, team leads, or coaches. See Chapter 8 for more ideas on leadership in sustainable software development.

I also believe that an attempt to build a successful culture is enhanced by the presence of at least one *level 5 leader* [Collins 2001]. These are the individuals who recognize that the greatest success is when they can help others succeed and give them the opportunity to receive the accolades they deserve, who view success as a team accomplishment and failure as a personal responsibility, not an opportunity to apportion blame on others. These people are few and far between and are unfortunately rarely promoted into senior management because they often lack the charisma, high-volume talking, and massive ego and self-confidence; the traits most often associated with getting ahead in the corporate world.

Visionary and Tactical

Effective teams strive for the optimal balance between being visionary (thinking about the long term) and tactical (focusing on today's problems), and this balance changes over the course of the project. In the early phases of a project there should be a heavier emphasis on being visionary, and in latter phases the emphasis should be placed on tactics related to finishing the project. Projects fail when there is too much emphasis on being visionary late in the development cycle or when there is too much emphasis on tactical issues too early in the project. Great teams are able to balance the two at each moment in the project.

Shared Sense of Urgency

In sustainable development it is important that everyone on the team shares the same sense of urgency to complete the project. If the business people are worried about the competition and the developers are more concerned about the perfect architecture, failure will result.

A shared sense of urgency is also the most important factor in building teams. It isn't compatible personalities or team building exercises or even necessarily mutual respect that make the best teams, it's a shared goal or aggressive but achievable deadline that the team uses as a rallying cry for getting the project done.

Highly Collaborative

Collaboration is a vital success factor in sustainable development. Good teams are able to work together, embrace the differences between personalities and roles, and strive for a successful project. They also recognize that there are clear roles for each of them to play. Businesspeople don't write software and programmers don't write business plans. Collaboration should be like breathing; it is always there and is done almost subconsciously. And it should be done in person (as opposed to e-mail or voice mail) as much as possible because that is the most effective form of collaboration.

Complementary Talents and Skills

Great cultures recognize talents and skills as separate from each other. Too many companies are focused on skill alone and recruit only for skills. But skills can be taught, whereas talent can't. Software development is a perfect example because people who are talented at complex problem solving make excellent programmers. Excellent programmers can learn new programming languages in a short period of time and will over time outperform their peers. And yet, most job ads in our industry still look for a certain number of years of experience programming in a particular language when what they should be looking for are people who are talented problem solvers.

Continually Improving and Learning

Continual improvement and learning is a vital element of sustainable development. Great people and teams continually learn and refine their projects and how they approach the projects. They use short time increments (many times per year) to ensure their pace is high and lightweight and use techniques to monitor progress, keep themselves on track, and introduce changes as required.

Change Tolerant

Great teams understand that change is necessary and desirable. They also understand that change must sometimes be made in the face of conflicting or incomplete information. However, they also realize that just because a decision is made at one point in time does not mean that it can't be or won't be modified as new information is available. Hence, being change tolerant also means that sometimes some extra work must be done at the current time so that change tolerance is possible in the future as well.

Risk-Aware

Risk is a constant element of all projects. Effective teams are always aware of risk, are able to differentiate between real and perceived risk, and are not afraid to make decisions with the best information possible in the face of risk. They are also constantly looking for ways to reduce or alleviate risk.

Fun

You can't always choose what you do, but you *can* choose how you do it [Lundin et al 2000]. Good people and teams recognize this. They find ways to make work more fun for their co-workers and customers.

Summary

Mindset and culture are more important than practices. Unfortunately, culture is not something that can be turned on and off like a light. Luckily, there is a spectrum of possible ideal cultures. What might work in one environment and with one set of team members will not necessarily work in a different environment with different people.

Creating the ideal culture takes a lot of hard work, and it takes people dedicated to making it happen—good people. The vast majority of people want to succeed and have the tools required to do so, if they are put into the right environment. There must be a shared sense of purpose and vision, and this is why there must be an effort made to getting the people with the right attributes onto the team and others off the team, or on the bus as in *Good to Great* [Collins 2001]. It's how the people in the team apply themselves to creating the necessary environment that separates the poor team from the average from the good and from the great team. There is an element of luck and being in the right place at the right time with the right people. Applying the principles and practices outlined in this book and thinking about your desired culture should get your team well on the way to a thriving, positive culture.

The rest of this book describes some of the recommended practices that support the four principles of sustainable development. There is a chapter for each principle, and each chapter explains in detail the rationale behind the principle and the practices that help to make it real.

Chapter 4

Working Product

A working product at all times should be the ultimate goal for every software team. The further a product is away from being in a working state and the longer it is in that state, the greater the time required to get the product back to a working state.

Software products need to be in a working state at all times. This could be called *virtually shippable* because the product could be shipped after a short period of verification testing and stabilization, the shorter the better. A working product does not mean that the product is feature complete or that all features are done; rather, that it can be shown to or given to a customer for use with the minimum possible number of unexplainable errors. The closer a team can get to continually keeping its product in a working state, the better the chances that its efforts can be maintained over time because of the level of discipline required and also because having a working product imparts greater flexibility and agility.

Why Working Product and Not Working Software?

I use the term working *product* and not the more common phrase working *software* deliberately. This is because from the customers' point of view, they rarely receive *just* software. Software is almost always accompanied by explicit deliverables such as documentation plus supporting infrastructure like a web site for information, updates, and support. There are also implicit deliverables such as an expectation that there has been testing before the customer sees the product. Hence, I use the term working product to encompass all the explicit and implicit deliverables and to reinforce the requirement for multi-functional collaboration within a team where software is one important part, but not the only part.

A working product is an underpinning of agile software development. Agile development demands the ability to get continual customer feedback, and the only way to get feedback on features and to keep customers interested in working with the product is to provide the customers a working product on a regular basis. A working product is a demonstration to customers that *this* is a product they can rely on. It is extremely difficult to keep customers interested in using a product if they develop a low opinion of it because it is unreliable, crashes, and has unpredictable problems and regressions (where features they depend on no longer work). Regressions are particularly dangerous, and one important aspect of having a working product is that nothing should be added to the product until the regression is fixed.

A working product also gives the product team an incredible amount of flexibility, not only in being able to change directions, but also in taking the latest version of software and shipping it at any time with the critical feature(s) the market demands. This flexibility translates into a sense of power for the development team derived from feeling in control and using that control to respond to changing situations.

The working product principle is a deliberate contrast to the traditional *code-then-fix* method of software development. This method, which is probably the most commonly used method of software development, is the practice of developing a feature and then debugging and altering the code until the feature works. When software is developed in short iterations of two to six weeks as in agile software development, the temptation is to believe that it is acceptable to apply *code-then-fix* in each iteration. However, the problem with the *code-then-fix* method is that teams are forced to waste time and effort debugging, effort that should be applied to satisfying customer problems. Wasted effort is a lost opportunity. Hence, having a working product every day and fixing defects as you go minimizes wasted effort and allows teams to focus on their customers. It also dramatically reduces the buildup of technical debt in the product, because chances are very high that problems are caught as soon as possible. As explained in Chapter 5, this requires a change in mentality about software development: All attempts must be made to *prevent* defects from reaching people, whether they are testers or customers.

In order to keep a product in a working state, teams need to focus on the quality of everything they do. Achieving this level of product quality requires a great deal of discipline and focus on the part of the development team: focus on the quality of the product and the discipline to ensure that every software modification passes an extensive suite of automated tests, or it is removed from the product until it does pass the tests (see *Ruthless Testing* in Chapter 5). Whenever a product is in a non-working state and changes are still being made to it, the development team is literally *flying blind* and technical debt is accumulating; a debt that will have to be repaid later. This situation is a recipe for disaster because the cost of fixing problems increases with time, as does the probability that multiple problems will show up in the final product and be found at customer sites.

The Need to Address Quality Promptly

If your car gets a flat tire, you know that if you keep on driving without fixing the flat, the rim will need replacing, and then the axle, and then various body parts as they are ground down through contact with the pavement. Eventually, your car is going to need major repairs, and even when you do get it repaired, it will never be the same. Most people wouldn't even consider the option of *not* changing a flat tire on their car. Yet with software teams the severity of a problem and its consequences are not so obvious, so the temptation is there to just leave it even if it leads to more problems down the road.

In *Lean Software Development* [Poppendieck and Poppendieck 2003] the analogy is drawn with an assembly line used in a manufacturing plant. If a problem is found with what is being produced on the assembly line, a big flashing light goes off and production stops until the problem is fixed. Software teams may hate having to stop their work, but addressing quality concerns promptly is a critical part of keeping a product in a working state while minimizing the effort required to keep it in that state.

A useful conversation to have with a product team is around the question *What would it take for us to ship our product every day to our customers?* In this case *ship* could mean providing daily updates or a complete new version of the software to install. The purpose of answering this question is to get the team thinking about minimizing the overhead activities that occur after the software is declared complete and can then be shipped to customers. The answers should be enlightening, because they will highlight not only all the changes the team will have to make but also the *ripple effect* this would have on the team's surrounding organization. Here are a few of the topics that might come up:

- *Quality assurance and testing become critical issues.* How are you going to keep the level of quality high in your software? If you are going to ship every day, a person can't do all your testing. You're going to have to automate as much testing as possible, and this likely means designing the product and product features for testability as opposed to thinking about testing after. And where people are required for testing you're going to have to ensure that they are available when they are needed, not working on another project.
- How much validation testing must take place on the final version of the product before the team and its customers have enough confidence in the product that it can be fully deployed? How many of the current validation tests could be automated and run every night or on a more frequent basis so that the testing is essentially done much earlier?
- Is your documentation and web site going to be ready to reflect the new changes every day? Most likely you're going to have to work out some automated way of updating the web site while ensuring that product documentation can be loaded off the Internet and not just the local hard drive (i.e., updated live).
- What happens when a customer finds a problem? How is he going to report it to you? How are you going to prioritize customer reports so that urgent fixes are made as rapidly as possible? How are you going to minimize the chances that a defect is fixed (reliably) without breaking something else?
- When a customer reports a problem to you, one of the first things she is going to want to know is what the status of the fix is. Are you going to let the customers review the status of their defect reports online and see when they can expect fixes?
- How are you going to develop features that take a long time (weeks to months) to complete? Most definitely the wrong answer is to wait

until the feature is complete before merging it into the source code. You are going to have to find a way to integrate these features in piecemeal while ensuring the product still works and while telling users what to expect every day, and you're going to have to find ways to get input from customers on the new features as they progress.

- *What if a critical feature breaks in a daily release?* Customers would have to be able to easily report the problem to you *and* back up to the previous day's version while they wait for a fix. This is the time when you will have to demonstrate responsiveness to your customers, because the time they spend waiting for a fix or backing up to the previous version costs them time and money.

The goal in this exercise is to ship the product to customers as frequently as possible. Shipping frequently encourages teams to minimize their overhead while maximizing their productivity; so they can ship frequently AND implement the features that their customers need. This is only possible by focusing on a working product, because by doing so teams will have to be ultra-efficient at finding, fixing, and *preventing* failures, as explained in Chapter 5. Teams that are able to achieve the frequent ship/features balance will consistently outinnovate teams that have one or more delays as they try to fix the problems that prevent their product from being in a working state.

Shipping daily is the ultimate goal, but there may be factors that make it possible to ship once a week or once a month. What you want to avoid is being able to ship only a couple of times a year. Note that it's one thing to ship twice a year and quite another to only be *able* to ship twice a year! Not all of your products need to get installed by all possible users, it is simply important to get the software installed and used on real problems as frequently as possible. Many open source projects and a smattering of commercial products are able to actually ship every day or at least very frequently. A few examples are:

- Eclipse (http://www.eclipse.org) is an open-source IDE project from IBM. A reliable update mechanism is built into the software so that updates can be made at any time.
- Qt (http://www.trolltech.com) is a commercial GUI cross-platform toolkit.

- Renderware (http://www.renderware.com) is a commercial game engine produced by Criterion that ships weekly.
- Torque (http://www.torque.com) is an inexpensive but high-quality game engine that is virtually open source.
- Microsoft regularly provides updates to the Windows operating system and Office tools. Although Microsoft makes an easy target for many people, I think it's worth pointing out that, overall, its updates work.
- Norton Anti-Virus is a common desktop tool that is updated whenever a new virus has been detected on the Internet.

Think of shipping every day from a purely technological standpoint. We have the technology right now in the Internet and binary update mechanisms to actually perform live updates of customer software as the developers merge their changes into the product, which would essentially entail multiple software updates every day. There are many reasons why we don't do this; I think the biggest is simply the *baggage* that the software industry is carrying around: that software quality is poor and updates should be done carefully or only after some (usually long) period of verification testing. There are clearly cases where verification and extreme caution before installation of a new software version is mandatory: for software systems where a software error could cause a person or other living thing to be injured or killed, the economy to collapse, or an expensive piece of equipment to be permanently disabled or destroyed. Clearly, these mission-critical software systems shouldn't be installed without a great deal of caution.

The problem today is that the vast majority of software produced today is *not* mission-critical, yet the software industry has done such a good job of training its users to expect poor quality that they expect to not be able to continue to do their work when they perform a simple software upgrade. Consider a commercial business that has a production pipeline made up one or more software products. The amount of confidence this business would have in being able to upgrade a product while people are working on a project is nil today. But, what if a production pipeline *could* be changed during a project? And frequently changed? What is the advantage to the software team that could offer this ability to its customers? *That* is the power of having a working product.

All the practices recommended in this chapter help project teams concentrate on keeping their product in a working, virtually shippable, state. Having a singular focus on a working product should be a rallying cry for every project team, one that will lead to significant positive team morale and a sense of ongoing accomplishment and ability to be proactive not reactive (i.e., in control). Achieving a working product is *not* extra work if it is done every day!

Ship at Unpredictable Times

One of the chief advantages of having a working product is being able to ship at unpredictable times. I saw a project a while ago where the requirement came in to ship a Japanese version of the shipping product. A large deal with a software distributor was at stake; the distributor needed to get the Japanese version within a month or the opportunity would be missed for another year.

The problem is that team members were in the middle of a development cycle for the new version of the product. One of the key architectural changes they had made for the new version was to internationalize the product because they anticipated the need for a Japanese version. However, because the architecture had changed quite a bit from what was currently shipping, they could not *port* the changes back to the shipping version. In a typical development team, this situation would cause a great deal of panic (and a missed opportunity). Luckily, this wasn't a typical team. Their solution to the problem was to take the software they were working on, *turn off all the new features* so the software was functionally identical to the shipping version, then complete the localization. The end result was a Japanese version of the product in less than two weeks; the English to Japanese translation and testing took more time than the engineering work!

This is one example of the power of having a working product. Having a working product put this team in control of its situation and allowed the flexibility and confidence to ship when it wanted.

Be Wary of Artificial Milestones

One of the teams I worked with had a *functionality freeze* milestone where all new features for the release had to be integrated into the product before the functionality freeze date.

The intention of the milestone was good (largely to ensure that the product could be documented with the features in a stable state and to ensure there was adequate time to test and stabilize the final product before shipping). However, for most features, the functionality freeze came too early in the schedule. As a result, developers would often postpone bugfixing until after the milestone, or they would check in incomplete features and sometimes just code stubs so that the feature would appear to be there and could then be fixed up during the bugfixing phase! Also, team leaders would encourage developers to postpone bugfixing until after the milestone so the features could be completed.

Hence, with artificial milestones (as with many practices), it is important to watch out for unintended side effects. In the case of the functionality freeze milestone, the emphasis on all development work before the milestone was on getting features into the code base, not on ensuring that the software still functioned.

On this product, the software would often be in an unshippable state for as much as six or nine months out of every year! Although it was tempting for teams to think they'd made terrific progress at the milestone ("Just look at all the features we checked in!") all hell would break loose after the milestone as the team would gallantly try to get the software back to a shippable state, with the end result that many defects couldn't be fixed due to a lack of time.

Even worse, many of the features would have to be removed or have the user interface disabled just to get the software working again. A great deal of effort was wasted, not only in fixing all the defects long after they were first introduced and getting the software working again, but in all the features that were implemented but never shipped.

Due to the chaos, each product release had slightly lower quality than the release before it. The end result was a gradual degradation of the software's quality over time and a rapid accumulation of an ever-increasing backlog of defects. This in turn led to longer *bugfix death marches* in every release, where even though the team was working hard to fix all the bugs, it never caught up. Because there were so many bugs, the feature freeze milestone was forced earlier for more stabilization time at the end of the release cycle. And, of course, the pressure to develop new features never went away.

The development team literally felt trapped because it had to choose between spending additional time bugfixing and less time developing features, or focus on developing new features and fixing fewer defects. They were also spending an incredible amount of time in their defect tracking system sorting, prioritizing, and analyzing defects. This is part of a classic software development death spiral described in Chapter 2, one that stifles the ability of the team to be innovative and agile.

Note that I'm *not* using this example to imply that milestones are bad, just that milestones need to be treated with caution. There is nothing wrong with a functionality freeze milestone, for example. The team that I describe above still uses the milestone, but its use is more rational. If you feel that this milestone is necessary for your project, then you should challenge each other to ensure that functionality freeze is as *late* as possible in the release cycle. The problem comes when people get too conservative and start believing in the milestones rather than in each other, or they emphasize the milestone over quality and stability.

PRACTICE 1: No "Broken Windows"

This practice could also be thought of as "no hacks or ugly workarounds." It is possible to think of many metaphors for this practice. The authors of *The Pragmatic Programmer* [Hunt and Thomas 2000] use the metaphor of a house for software development, where once a house has a broken window, the occupants of the house will tend to be careless and more prone to leaving broken windows themselves. Another metaphor for this practice is counter space in your kitchen: All it takes is for someone to leave an unopened letter on a section of your counter, and before you know it, there will be more there. Software has all the same properties as a house or kitchen countertop: It's exceedingly easy to make changes in a sloppy, haphazard way. Once one sloppy change has been made, others will follow; this is unfortunately human nature. Therefore, never start the decay, and if you find some bad code, clean it up immediately. If the programmer who left the mess behind is still working on the code, make sure he or she knows about the cleanups you have made and why you made them; peer pressure to write good code is a good thing.

In software, once decay has started, the decay will continue and get worse over time. It is really hard to care about leaving the code in a good state when there are obvious signs of neglect. This is unfortunately human nature, and the best way to combat human nature is to always leave the code in a better state than when you started. Don't leave a mess behind for someone else to clean up! Ugly workarounds cause problems and are a symptom that the product is most likely not in a working state.

Imagine That Your Customer Can See Your Broken Windows

I learned the importance of having no broken windows early in my career. The company I was working for at the time depended on a software product that had been written by another company that went bankrupt. Luckily, we were able to get the source code so that we didn't have to develop a similar product ourselves. I was given the responsibility of keeping this software working.

This source code was littered with comments like:

```
// Ugly workaround to fix the case where the index
// is negative.  Be sure to fix this in version 3!!
//
```

At first, I found it frustrating to read these comments and to fix problems that had never been properly resolved in the first place. But after a while, I developed a sense of empathy for the original developers. No doubt they had been under a great deal of time pressure, and I suspect they would have been embarrassed if they knew that one of their *customers* had to deal with this code.

This experience taught me that while being under extreme time pressure *may* be a valid reason for leaving a broken window, there are *no* valid reasons to leave it there for anything more than a few days.

PRACTICE 2: Be Uncompromising about Defects

It is vital that you adopt an uncompromising attitude toward defects. The goal is to avoid a defect backlog, where there is a list of open defects that is too large for the team to deal with immediately. Defect backlogs are evil and must be avoided because:

- Defect backlogs burden teams with repetitive searching, sorting, and categorizing tasks that waste time and take away from productive work.
- A backlog, by definition, means that more defects are being carried around than can be reasonably dealt with. The number of defects

makes it more difficult to find the defects that *must* be fixed, the defects that customers repeatedly encounter and can't work around.

- A defect backlog is a strong indicator that new features are being developed on top of defective code.
- The larger the backlog, the greater the chance the backlog is never going to be eradicated. I have seen cases where teams were carrying around backlogs that would take over a year to fix, even if all they did was fix bugs and no new problems were introduced!
- The larger the backlog, the greater the chance that defects are going to be shipped to customers and that customers will find defects that they can't work around, so you're going to have to send them a patch. This is expensive for you and your customer.
- The greater the time between when a defect is introduced and when it is fixed, the greater the cost of fixing it. Carrying a backlog thus means that you are implicitly accepting higher costs of development and future change.

How to Avoid a Defect Backlog

- Be ruthless: When a defect is reported, decide as quickly as possible to either fix it or get rid of it, preferably by marking it with a special state to indicate that it won't be fixed along with an explanation as to why. This way you won't lose the information.
- Fix regressions, where a feature that used to work stops working, immediately. Regressions put the product into an unknown state where users won't be able to trust it and developers won't be able to make changes with confidence. To achieve sustainable development, regressions must be fixed immediately, *before any other changes are made* to the product, even if that means that work on some new feature must be stopped to fix the regression.
- Once you have decided to fix a defect, do so as quickly as possible, and for as many defects as you can manage. Understand what caused them and how to prevent them in the future.
- Fix all the known defects in a new feature before moving on to work on the next feature. Then, once you move on to the next feature, be ruthless with any newly reported defects.

The Value of Being Uncompromising

I have worked on and with quite a few teams that were uncompromising with defects. The common thread in all these teams was that the number of known defects in our product was *constant to slightly decreasing* over time, even as we added new features and rewrote large sections of the code. Every team used different techniques and practices to accomplish this. What mattered was the mindset.

Put More Effort into Defect *Prevention* Than Bugfixing

The most important point about being ruthless about defects is that you need to put more effort into *preventing* defects than into fixing them. Defect detection is still vital; it's just that defect prevention is even more important. Being ruthless about defects and trying to avoid the accumulation of a backlog is one thing, but if your product doesn't have safeguards in place to prevent defects from getting to your QA department or customers, then you are still going to get a backlog, no matter how fast you fix and classify your defects. Defect prevention is described in detail in Chapter 5.

Use a Defect Tracking Database, but Don't Build It Yourself!

Being ruthless about defects, of course, assumes your team is using a defect tracking system. If you don't have one, there are many good commercial, free, and open source systems that can be downloaded and installed pretty quickly if you don't want to purchase one. A good example is bugzilla (http://www.bugzilla.org/). Because there are so many decent defect systems available today, this is a perfect example of a tool that should never be developed internally. Focus on what makes your product unique and on shipping it!

Being Pragmatic about Defects

If you are starting a project with known technical debt or are concerned that your product quality may slip, there are a few things you can do:

- Insert bug fix-only iterations between feature development iterations. If product quality is slipping, you'd be surprised by how many users appreciate a stable product with a few focused features.
- Set some quality-related *exit criteria* for your iterations. Then, set the rule that the team can't call an iteration complete until the exit criteria are met. An example exit criterion might be "There can be no 'stop ship' defects in the product and no known regressions." Another might be "There can be no known open and unresolved defects" (to reinforce the need to be ruthless). These exit criteria add some extra discipline to iterative development through having a clear goal.
- A variant on the previous point is to let the team decide (the team includes the users or user representatives!) when the quality is good enough to move on to the next iteration.

These ideas might cause some people to balk, but I think you need to do what is best for your project. Your goal is to ship repeatedly, and with the least amount of wasted effort. I have used or seen each of the above suggestions on various projects, and they work. However, you do need to be careful, because you should not need to regularly rely on these nor use them for any extended period of time; disciplined iterative development alone should be sufficient.

PRACTICE 3: "Barely Sufficient" Documentation

In order for teams to concentrate on a working product, they should minimize the amount of time spent writing documents that are not part of the product. Examples of this type of document are requirements and design documents[1].

---

1. *Internal* documentation is distinct from the *external* documentation that is included with the software. External documentation such as help and feature documentation is required by customers and should be considered as features. The intent of this practice is to minimize the internal documentation only.

Barely sufficient documentation is another important part of agile development. All too often, teams forget why they produce documentation: to produce a working product. In too many cases, documentation is *required* before a project can proceed to the next step. This introduces a linearity to development that is unhealthy and unrealistic. Many people lose sight of the fact that what truly matters in any development project is the process, especially the conversations and decisions required to produce a useful product. Documents are secondary to collaboration and learning and are a *result* of the process, not its focus.

This practice is intended to encourage teams to focus on what matters the most: their working products. If you have been involved in or observed a project where the team spent months or years trying to understand user requirements and writing documents without ever producing a product (or even writing any code at all), you'll understand the reasoning behind this rule! Customers don't know what they want until they see it; documents don't help customers at all.

Minimal Documentation and Code Comments

Some people carry the drive for minimal documentation too far. One example is code comments, where some individuals claim that code comments are superfluous because (a) when automated tests are present, code documentation adds very little and (b) most code comments are extra work that don't add value.

I think this is a dangerous attitude because good comments aid the understandability of code. Many of the best programmers I know write the comments first and describe the logic of what they are doing and then they write the code. So, while it's true that comments that state the obvious aren't valuable, it's important to not dismiss all comments.

Some of the barely sufficient forms of key documentation are:

- The use of *index cards* for feature description in cycle planning. Index cards are used to describe features, to record the essential facts, and encourage team members to discuss the details. They also give team members something tangible to hold in their hands and quickly move around during planning sessions.

- The collection of *feature cards* for a project should serve as adequate documentation of requirements. It may be necessary in exceptional cases to provide additional documentation, but these should be truly exceptional circumstances not the norm.
- Design your software collaboratively in front of a *whiteboard*. Great discussions almost always result that highlight problems and alternative approaches. Then, simply take a picture of the whiteboard when done and place the image on a web page.
- An alternative to drawing a design on a whiteboard is to use a *sketching tool*. There are some good inexpensive tools available, such as SketchBook Pro from Alias (http://www.alias.com).
- *Put design details like relationships and code rationale with the source code* (where it can be easily kept up to date) *and extract them* using a tool like JavaDoc or doxygen. This is a good practice because it encourages collaboration and decision making over document writing in addition to encouraging teams to get on to developing their product.

For details on designing software in an agile development context, refer to the section *Simple Design* in Chapter 6 on Design Emphasis.

The examples given above of barely sufficient documentation are by necessity brief and far from exhaustive. An entire book [Ambler and Jeffries 2002] has been written on this topic, and interested readers should refer to it for further information.

The Dangers of Excessive Documentation

I can think of two prominent examples of teams I have worked in that did not understand the practice of minimal documentation.

One case was early in my career where I worked at a company with a heavyweight development process. There was a rigorous process where for every feature we had to produce, in series: a requirements document, a functional specification, a design document, and written test plans. We had a large set of bookshelves where all these documents were kept. Review meetings were held for each document. It was amazing that we got any work done! We moved very slowly and wasted a lot of time writing, reviewing, and pushing documents around.

And some of our priorities were rather bizarre: I remember one meeting where there was a debate about whether we should use round bubbles or ellipses in design documents. And I'm sure you can guess how much these documents were consulted after we'd moved on to other features…!

Another example I can think of was a team that was charged with building a next-generation version of an existing product. There was a desire to build something different that would leapfrog the competition. This team spent six months trying to identify user requirements and designing what a next-generation product should look like architecturally. The result? A team leader, two senior software developers, two other developers, a user representative, and a high-profile customer produced quite a few documents and no code, not even a prototype, before the project was cancelled! That was a wasted opportunity, and a ton of wasted effort, and the need for the new product is still there today.

PRACTICE 4: Continuous Integration

An important team discipline is to continuously integrate changes together. Frequent integration helps to ensure that modules that must fit together will, and also that the product continues to work with all the changes. Many developers have the bad habit of checking out a number of files and not checking them in again until their work is done, often days or weeks later. Developers should integrate their work every day, or even better, many times per day. This gradual introduction of changes ensures that integration problems or regressions are caught early, in addition to naturally allowing multiple developers to work on the same section of the source code. Of course, in order to catch problems it is important that your team has automated tests in place to help catch integration problems as explained in Chapter 5.

PRACTICE 5: Nightly Builds

In order for your team to ensure that your software is working, it should be completely rebuilt from scratch one or more times per day. The build should include as many automated tests as possible to catch integration problems early, and the result of the build should be an installable product image. Nighttime is a good time to do this because no one is working on the code, and there are plenty of idle computers available. However, if you can do it, there is a lot of benefit to building the product as many times per day as possible. If the build or tests fail, fix the problems first thing in the morning and don't let anyone integrate any additional work until after the build succeeds again, otherwise there is a risk of multiple bad changes accumulating that will jeopardize the quality of the product.

Nightly Builds and Configuration Management

Ensure that all assets required to build and test a project are stored in your CM tool. An excellent test is to regularly start from a "clean slate": remove everything associated with your project from your disk, get the latest version of all the files by checking them out, do a complete build, and ensure that all the automated tests still run. The best time to run this test is every night, as part of your product's nightly build.

*Store your **entire** project in your CM tool.* If your project includes user documentation, web pages, demo content, etc., make sure it is **all** in your CM tool. Too often, the project team will only focus on its software, but very few projects consist only of software. This can cause problems when it comes time to integrate the various pieces because manual work is often required to gather everything together and then verify that all the pieces are still compatible. No manual work is required if all the parts of the project are kept together and the entire project is built every night. You should never accept separate build processes and multiple integration steps.

Pay Attention to Build Times

You should always keep an eye on the product build times. The faster you can keep the build, the faster the feedback you'll get when you need to quickly generate a cut of the product. Long build times encourage developers to take potentially dangerous shortcuts and also to pay less attention to keeping the problem under control.

Long build times are almost always an indicator that something is wrong with the structure of the product: too many interdependencies between modules, not enough modules, or worst of all, duplicated or unnecessary code. In languages like C or C++ there might also be "include file" bloat, with include files making unnecessary #include statements or declaring inline functions that should be moved to the .cpp file.

Here's an example of the most common problem:

```
// File: A.h

// This class contains a member variable that is a pointer
to an
// instance of another class.
//
#include "B.h"

class A {
    ...
    protected:
    class B *m_Bptr;
    ...
}
```

The problem with this seemingly innocent class is the #include of "B.h," which is the file that declares "class B." If this file that declares "class A" (A.h) is included in many places in your product, build time will suffer because the preprocessor is going to spend a great deal of time processing A.h AND B.h, when in fact B.h is not necessary because a forward declaration can be used in A.h and an include of B.h only added to the .cpp files that actually need to use "m_Bptr":

```
// File: A.h

// This class contains a member variable that is a pointer
// to an instance of another class.
//
class B;    // All class A needs is a forward declaration of
            // class B.
```

```
class A {
    ...
    protected:
    class B *m_Bptr;
    ...
}
```

> **TIP** **Timestamp the start and end of all builds.**
> A good practice to follow is to timestamp the start and end of
> all complete builds and keep a log. Then, write a simple script
> to catch large increases in build time. If possible, produce a
> simple chart that can then be put on a web page and quickly
> viewed. It's always easier to glance at a chart than to dig
> through a log file!

The Entire Team Owns the Product Build

It should be part of the team's mindset that it is everyone's responsibility to pay attention to the product build. Unfortunately, some developers I have encountered feel that cheaper labor should be hired to look after the builds. This attitude is wrong and unprofessional. It is wrong because the cheaper labor won't know the code and won't be able to fix any problems when they're found—only the actual developers can do so. It is unprofessional, because hiring someone else to do part of your job is like a mechanic hiring someone else to look after his tools…!

PRACTICE 6: Prototyping

Making a conscious effort to prototype solutions to risky problems helps to increase the chance of having a working product. Prototypes are an inexpensive way to try out ideas so that as many issues as possible are understood before the real implementation is made. There are two main classes of prototypes that you can use to positively impact your product. The first is the true prototype, where a test implementation is used to understand a problem before it is implemented for real. The second is the notion of "tracer bullets" [Hunt and Thomas 2000].

Reducing risk is a key part of working software. You need to continually assess risk in collaborative planning sessions, but, most importantly, when key risks are identified, you need to *do* something as early as possible in the project to ensure the risk is well understood. Prototypes are an extremely effective and relatively inexpensive way to evaluate risks. Not only do you gain an understanding of the nature of the risk, you have a prototype of a solution to the problem and hence have much greater confidence that you understand the length of time required to address the problem. You also have an implementation you can borrow from, even if it is only ideas, when implementing the complete solution.

Prototypes Don't Need to Always Be Software

I once worked on a project where we used a large number of prototypes, and few of them were implemented in software. Very early in the project we found ourselves struggling to provide an interface that our target users could easily understand and learn in a couple of minutes. Our first attempt was implemented in software, which took us several weeks to implement. After getting a few users to try out the software, it was painfully obvious that we had gotten the interface horribly wrong. It was confusing and required users to learn the quirks of the software not work naturally. We wanted to try again but were afraid to do so because we felt that:

(a) It would take the same amount of time to implement a new prototype.
(b) After our first experience, we had little confidence that we could get it right the second time.
(c) We felt that anywhere from two to ten more attempts might be required to get it right.

For this problem, we were lucky enough to have an excellent usability person on the team. She suggested that we try out a whiteboard and paper prototype, so we spent a few hours laying out the interface on a whiteboard and putting together a number of large sticky notes for buttons, pull-down menus, etc. Then we asked some users to work through a sample problem while we manually made sure that the whiteboard interface updated in a realistic way. It took us a few more of these prototypes to find the optimal solution, but this took us only a couple of days. I suspect we saved ourselves more than two months of engineering effort!

Throwaway Prototypes

A throwaway prototype is an excellent tool to evaluate risky features and develop better time estimates for a feature. As explained in the "iterative development" section, the elimination of risk as early as possible in a project is often a critical project success factor. Doing a quick prototype in a small number of iterations is often an excellent way to acquire a much better understanding of the problem and the actual risk. Also, by developing the prototype as a throwaway, usually in a copy or branch of the product or a simple prototype application, it is easy to ensure that the product is still in a working state when the real solution to the problem is implemented.

Quite simply, a prototype is a *quick and dirty* implementation that explores key target areas of a problem. Prototypes should not be production ready, nor should they provide a complete implementation of the desired solution. They might even be implemented in a scripting language like Python or Ruby to save time. The bottom line with prototypes is that they should be used as a point of reference only when implementing the complete solution to a problem.

One of the downsides of prototypes is that you often have to show them to customers and management in order to demonstrate progress. One of the conclusions your audience could draw, if you are not careful, is that the problem is solved and done when, in fact, all you have is a rough proof of concept. If you do show a prototype to customers, be sure they know what you are showing them *before* you show it to them to avoid situations where your audience thinks the problem is solved. You could also make it obvious through rough visual output that clearly does not look done.

A good analogy to use is car design. The car manufacturers all regularly produce concept cars to try out ideas or demonstrate a proof of concept. These cars are one-offs that could be turned into a production version fairly quickly, but they are definitely not ready for shipping to customers. Likewise, many product designers ensure that if they are showing a digital prototype such as a rendered image to their clients that the image does not make the product look *done*. If you suspect there is going to be pressure to use the prototype for the shipping product, it might be better to consider using *tracer bullets* instead.

"Tracer Bullets"

"Tracer Bullets" are a deliberate approach that uses a prototype that is intended from the outset to gradually turn into the final solution [Hunt and Thomas 2000]. The analogy is combat: Imagine you have to shoot at and hit a target in complete darkness. The brute force approach would be to point your gun in the right direction and hope for the best. However, a more effective approach is to use glowing rounds called tracer bullets. You start by firing a few tracer bullets and then correcting your aim until you can fire real bullets to destroy the target. In the real world, tracer bullets are every few bullets in a clip. Hence, the software analogy is that if you're uncertain you're pointing in the right direction, start by building a viable prototype and keep adding to it until your customer says, "That's it!" This is really a microcosm of agile development, where multiple short iterations are used to continually add to a prototype. The difference is that agile development is applied to a collection of features (a whole product) and tracer bullets can be used on one feature, problem, or area of risk.

PRACTICE 7: Don't Neglect Performance

Performance is one topic that generates passionate discussions in software development. Some people feel that code clarity is more important and that you should get the code clarity right first and then optimize the 1 to 3 percent of code that needs it. Others feel that you should code for performance first, because if you don't, your code will always be slow.

Personally, I get scared when a development team or developer says "we'll worry about performance later." I have seen too many projects where the team felt the need to get the features in before worrying about performance led to months or years of rework. Code clarity *does* come first, but not at the expense of performance. This is another case where you need to embrace the genius of the AND: You must be concerned with performance AND clarity, with a strong bias toward the latter. You don't have to be obsessive about performance, but you need to understand what the customer's expectations are, design for the right level of performance from the beginning and where performance really matters, ensure that you have tests to measure performance and let you know when the performance degrades in a noticeable way (see Chapter 5 for more on performance tests). You should never have to hear from your customers that your product is too slow...!

I also get scared when a development team says its software will get faster on the next generation of hardware. The fact that computers are getting faster is a constant and everyone benefits, including your competitors. Applications are also getting larger and more complex. You need to understand at least the basics of performance for the programming language and framework your product works in. Just because you develop in Java, for example, doesn't mean that you can neglect performance, even though Java is an interpreted language.

Data Structures and Performance

Sometimes, even the simplest things like data structures can have a huge performance impact. For example, I once worked on a product where the code was copying three large arrays into a single buffer. One day we noticed that all of a sudden the application had gotten a *lot* slower. After profiling the code performance, we discovered that the size of the three arrays had been increased just enough so that they were each larger than the CPU's primary memory cache. Hence, every time one of the arrays was used (i.e., every byte) the CPU flushed its cache to make room for the new array. The solution was to use a single array, which could be quickly streamed into the CPU's memory cache by the hardware and then accessed much faster.

PRACTICE 8: Zero Tolerance for Memory and Resource Leaks

If you develop in a programming language or environment where memory or resource leaks are possible, you must have zero tolerance for leaks. Resource leaks lead to unpredictable behavior such as program crashes, and they can also be exploited by hackers to compromise your customer's computers.

I wish it were possible to say that this is an easy practice to follow. Unfortunately, the reality is that even if you use available tools (see Chapter 5 on Defect Prevention), leaks can still happen. Sometimes, lower level APIs that your application uses leak memory. There isn't much you can do about those except to report the problem to the vendor. And while it might seem ideal to adopt a policy where you always free every allocated resource, sometimes you can't. The most frustrating example is if you have a large application that allocates large amounts of memory. Because operating systems don't provide a fast exit path for applications, if you were to explicitly free up all allocated memory when the application stops, it may take many seconds for the application to actually go away, which can be frustrating to users. Therefore, to get the appearance of a fast exit, it is common practice to not bother freeing up memory at all, quit, and let the operating system worry about it. This wouldn't be a problem except that when you use a memory leak detection tool, all of the memory and resources that were not explicitly freed on exit are reported as leaks, which makes legitimate leaks virtually impossible to detect…!

All I can advise is to at least make sure you exercise due diligence— don't just ignore trying to find leaks. The tools available today have APIs that you can hook up to your application to start and stop leak detection. These can be very useful.

No Memory Leak Can Be Ignored

A common misconception about memory leaks is that only the *big* ones matter. Unfortunately, this is not true; a leak as small as one byte of memory is enough to set up a *fence* in the application's memory pool that will ensure the system cannot reuse that memory. One of my favorite examples of this problem happened a few years ago…

I had just started at a company working on a product developed in C++ where it turned out the team had been very lax about memory leaks. Less than a month into the job I absent-mindedly left the application running at the end of the workday. When I came in the next morning, I discovered that the application had crashed sometime during the night. I wasn't sure it was a problem, thinking that perhaps the crash was caused by backups or some such thing, so that night I left it running again with the same result. Curious, I then wrote a simple script to monitor the system memory (using a system call) so I could log memory usage while running the application. What I discovered was normal memory usage in the form of spikes as the program allocated and properly freed up large chunks of memory, but overall the memory consumed increased at a constant pace. The culprit turned out to be a very small leak of 4 bytes that unfortunately was happening every time the cursor blinked!

Our users had been complaining that they had to constantly save their work because the application crashed at unpredictable times (sometimes unfortunately during a save operation). Once we understood the number of leaks in the product, we undertook a concerted effort to remove the leaks and released a version of the software with *no* new features, just all the leaks fixed. I insisted we do this despite the braying of our marketing department.

That release was one of the most satisfying releases I have ever done, because our customers gave the release rave reviews and applauded us for not adding features and just fixing their major complaint—stability. And after another release, our marketing department realized that although they hadn't been able to say anything new about the product, their job was now much easier because we had gained a reputation of listening to our customers, which is very powerful marketing indeed.

PRACTICE 9: Coding Standards and Guidelines

Make sure your team talks about what good code is and what coding practices team members like and dislike. Put them down on paper or in a web page and get everyone on the team to agree to them. Don't get hung up on silly formatting issues like whether curly braces should appear on the same line or next, just get everyone to agree that when they modify a file, they should follow the same formatting conventions. Having consistent coding conventions simply makes code easier to read. Plus, there is a huge benefit to having the team discuss good code and bad code; they can learn from each other and understand each other's viewpoints.

The Problem with Coding Standards and Guidelines

. . . Is that they are rarely, if ever, reread and updated by the team once they have been created. Once created, the standard is most useful for new people who join the team, so they can quickly understand some of the desirable coding traits for the project. I think this is fine, but it does reinforce the need to spend minimal time on creating the standard[2]. You can't force people to regularly read something they already know, and there is little point in trying to continually update the document; periodic updates should be all that is required. When it comes to understanding what is good code and how to recognize bad code, the greatest value to a team is the regular good code/bad code discussions and reading through each other's code because this *on-the-job* collaboration helps create shared understanding and learning. The lessons learned in the on-the-job collaboration are priceless and can't be captured on paper in coding guidelines or standards.

TIP   *Tune Coding Guidelines to the Team*
One of the teams I worked in had one coding guideline: Use whatever coding conventions you're comfortable with, but if you're modifying someone else's code, you have to follow his or her conventions.

This rule worked for that particular team because we all had many years of experience, and we each had our own coding conventions (and we were opinionated about them). We trusted each other to write good code and to be adaptable.

Our goal was simply to avoid problems like files being reformatted (to suite someone's taste who uses different conventions), variables being renamed (because of different naming conventions), and multiple conventions being used in the same file. We didn't want to waste time discussing or debating our coding conventions or making changes that had no functional purpose.

---

2. There are many good standards online, and these could serve as an excellent starting point.

PRACTICE 10: Adopt Standards (Concentrate on Your Value-Add)

Another way of stating this practice is *don't reinvent the wheel*. For every project you work on, you need to understand where your *value-add* is, and then ensure that you put as little effort as possible into portions of your project that are not *value-add* (i.e., plumbing). Reuse as much as you can for the plumbing, even if it isn't perfect; you can always modify or extend it to suit your needs.

One of the most significant changes to the software industry is taking place in open source software. I believe that everyone in the software industry (and not just developers!) needs to at least understand what open source software is available and what the different open source licenses mean. While only time will tell if open source makes software into purely a commodity (as some claim), it is clear that what open source *is* doing is changing our definition of what is plumbing and what is value-add. Too many teams spend too much effort developing code that is already readily available to them via open source. The challenge is for everyone to recognize the value of developing the plumbing in a community. Naturally, over time the definition of what is a commodity will change, and this is a natural and healthy progression toward being able to offer customers richer and more sophisticated solutions over time.

Open source software addresses the concern that when problems are found you are powerless to fix them. This is a common problem when commercial third-party libraries or components are used: If you find a problem, you are completely dependent on the provider of the library to fix it. If the provider doesn't or can't fix the problem in a timely manner, you often have to implement an ugly workaround. With open source, you can make the change and submit it to the community, where all the other users benefit.

IBM is an excellent example of understanding the difference between commodity and value-add. IBM took the bold move of developing its Eclipse IDE as an open source project, but IBM also uses Eclipse as a foundation for its own commercial products and allows third parties to develop their own commercial products on top of Eclipse. Being a free IDE has created a large community of developers who are comfortable with Eclipse and are also potential buyers of IBM's other tools.

XML is another example of the power of adopting standards. The use of XML has proliferated quickly because of the ease of use of the language and its supporting libraries. The ready availability of XML libraries and parsers means that today it is virtually impossible to justify designing a proprietary text-based file format and wasting time writing a parser for it. This is most definitely a good thing because it means that one more piece of the standard building blocks required by virtually all programs has been taken care of. XML frees developers to work on their value-add.

PRACTICE 11: Internationalize from Day One

Get in the habit of ensuring your products are internationalized[3] from day one. There is no extra overhead once you understand what is required. The bottom line is that the largest amount of economic growth globally in the next decade is projected to take place outside of English-speaking United States. The implication should be obvious: Your company needs to think globally, and so should you.

This practice applies to the need for a working product because of the discipline required. The process of continual localization as the product is changed is a discipline that, while sometimes burdensome, also requires discipline on the part of the project team and the skills learned through this discipline transfer to other areas of keeping the product in a working state.

Internationalization and a Working Product

Internationalization may seem like an odd practice to include with the principle of working software. I view this type of issue as part of the required mindset. You need to think about the critical things for the long-term success of your project that are trivial to do at the start of

---

3. Internationalization is the act of making software capable of displaying its user interface in multiple languages. Localization is the translation of the text strings into other languages. Software developers internationalize their software, while localization is usually done by a third-party translation service managed by the project team.

the project but if attempted later will severely destabilize it for a long period of time.

I have seen too many projects where internationalization was not considered until several years into the project. In each case, the architecture had become complicated enough that the work was considered extremely risky, and the project team continually argued against it or tried to suggest band-aid solutions or workarounds such as only localizing one small part of the product. Yet, for most of these projects, the business reality was that since the product was sold worldwide, it needed to have a multilingual interface. Eventually, the business interests won; the software changes were as disruptive as predicted and the result was a product that took a great deal of time to get back to a stable working state.

PRACTICE 12: Isolate Platform Dependencies

If your code must support multiple platforms, a clean separation between platform-specific code and all the other code is essential to have software that can be easily kept in a working state. Some examples of a *platform* are operating systems, graphics subsystems, runtime environments, libraries, and user interface toolkits. The best way to isolate platform dependencies is usually through an abstract interface (such as a Façade design pattern) so that the majority of the software is isolated from the platform-dependent code. Otherwise, software can become littered with conditional code that makes the code hard to maintain, debug, and port to other platforms in the future. If platform dependencies are important to your project, take the time to do them right. The effort will pay off.

Beware of Copy and Paste Porting

I have seen a number of very poor ports of code, especially to a new operating system. The problem is that the quickest way to do a port is to simply copy and paste the code, then make the changes required for the new platform.

The most extreme example I've seen of copy and paste porting was a project where the programmers duplicated the contents of *entire source files,* even if all that was different for the new platform was a few lines of code! The result was extra effort, since bug fixes were often made in only one copy of the code, or features were only added for one platform. It was also hard to know what was actually platform-specific. The result was more time spent coding and testing. In the end, we had to completely redo the port, and the second porting effort was harder than the first!

Admittedly, the previous example is an extreme one. But even on a smaller scale, copy and paste can still be a major impediment to keeping a product in a working state. For example, I remember one project where a product was first written for UNIX, then ported to Windows, and then to the Mac. Because the ports were not done at the same time, there were far too many cases where three copies of the same few lines of code were duplicated one after the other. The code was hard to read, maintain, and keep working. We had to do a major cleanup, which probably cost as much as the total of the original ports. All this effort could have been saved if the ports had been done properly, by isolating the platform dependencies behind suitable abstract interfaces.

Summary

Software products should always be in a shippable state. This does not mean a feature complete state. A working product gives teams the maximum possible flexibility and agility while minimizing wasted effort. The longer a product is in a nonworking state, the greater the effort required to return it to a working state. If problems are neglected too long, it may be impossible to return the product to a working state.

This chapter has outlined a number of practices related to keeping a product in a working state. By necessity, there are references to practices in other chapters because all the principles and practices described in this book reinforce each other. Subsequent chapters cover the principles of defect prevention, design, and continuous refinement. Defect prevention is required for working software because teams must have automated, *not* effort-wasting manual, methods to keep their products in a working state.

Likewise, in a complex environment of continual change, the design practices employed by the team must reinforce agility and changeability so that all hell does not break loose every time a change is made. The principle of continuous refinement is also vital for working software, because the project management practices used by the team must provide a lightweight and flexible way to continually monitor the project at frequent intervals to gauge progress and introduce the necessary changes to keep the project on track, and the product working.

Chapter 5

Defect Prevention

A focus on defect prevention over defect detection is an important principle of sustainable development. Defect detection follows what is probably the most common method used today to develop software: the *code-then-fix* mindset, where features are developed, testing is done (by users, a testing group, or Quality Assurance), and then defects are fixed. In this approach, there is a noticeable time lag between when defects are introduced and when they are actually fixed. Defect prevention by contrast follows the *code-then-fix* mindset, where features are developed using automated tests and related practices that catch the vast majority of defects when they are introduced so they can be fixed immediately when it is cheapest to do so. A profile that illustrates the difference between a defect prevention culture and a defect detection culture is shown in Figure 5-1.

Cheaper or Easier?

I've had some developers tell me, "It's cheaper to fix defects after they're found than it is to prevent them." These developers are deluding themselves and confusing cheaper with easier: It certainly *seems* easier to concentrate on getting features out the door, then worrying about fixing them up later. But what these people miss is that customers find many of the defects, and that is extremely expensive for your company and for your customers. Even more important, however, is that having to fix defects later causes the team to lose control of the project, and this loss of control directly impacts the ability to be agile.

Defect prevention in a chemical manufacturing plant is taking the pumps offline periodically to perform preventive maintenance. Pumps that are regularly maintained are less prone to breaking down, and by pro-actively maintaining their equipment, the plant employees are able

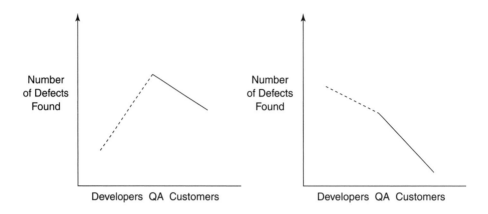

Figure 5-1
In a culture predominantly oriented around defect detection (left), the main burden for finding defects is placed on a quality assurance (or testing) organization, and quite a few defects are shipped to customers. However, in a defect prevention culture (right) the largest numbers of defects are found at the earliest possible moment, before the product reaches quality assurance, and very few defects are shipped to customers.

to avoid running from one crisis to another. They are in control of the situation, not victims of circumstance. A defect prevention mindset in software development should also result in being more in control than purely responding to events.

Defect prevention has real return on investment. Let's assume that the same number of design and coding errors are produced in a defect detection and prevention culture. In a defect detection culture, the majority of defects are found through manual testing and *after* code has been integrated into the product. On the other hand, in a defect prevention culture, the emphasis is on finding defects *before* integration into the product. The predominance of low-value manual testing and elaborate defect tracking systems in defect detection have a very real cost, as does the fact that there is a time delay between when a defect is introduced and when it is fixed. By contrast, in a defect prevention environment, the result of thorough automated testing, high-value manual testing, and fewer defects that reach customers more than offsets the cost of spending extra time in team collaboration and writing automated tests. An elaborate financial model could be developed, but hopefully a quick mental exercise should do.

Unfortunately, most software organizations emphasize defect detection and do very little in the way of defect prevention. There are some obvious symptoms of a defect detection oriented culture:

- Developers rely on testers/Quality Assurance/users to find defects in their products. Developers work on the software for a while, then they "toss it over the wall" to testers/QA, who toss it back when problems are found.
- A noticeable number of regressions are found by people (users or QA), where features that already existed stop working as expected when new changes are made. Regressions are a strong indicator that there is not enough testing and also that the product may need refactoring due to unexpected interdependencies, another indicator of technical debt.
- People believe that many tasks, including testing, are "beneath" highly paid programmers and are best done by lower paid help, so the developers can work on features (i.e., write code). While the features get done in the short term, the products these people work on get on the unsustainable development curve and quickly become more expensive to maintain and enhance over time.
- A backlog of defects that is carried over from release to release of the product. Defect backlogs are an indicator that technical debt is accumulating in the product, and they should be avoided at all costs. Once a team is faced with a backlog, the ongoing pressures to develop more features mean that the backlog is going to stay and will almost always continue to grow.
- Project team members spend inordinate amounts of time prioritizing, sorting, and viewing defect-related information. Defect backlogs are a huge drain on the time available to a project team. The less time spent doing the administrative chores in defect tracking, the better.
- An emphasis on the importance of bug tracking tools as *strategic* tools. Bug tracking tools are important, but they aren't strategic to your success. There are plenty of perfectly adequate systems available.

Another way to look at the type of culture is to ask your team the following question:

How would you prefer to find out about a serious defect?

(a) From your customer.
(b) From your QA department.
(c) Find it yourself.

In a defect prevention culture, your answer would be (c); in a defect detection culture it would be (b), with (a) as an outcome . . .

In a defect detection culture, developers have abdicated the responsibility of testing and product quality to other groups, usually QA. This is wrong, because developers control the processes and practices used to produce the product and because control is essential to agility.

The primary difference between a defect detection and defect prevention culture is the attitude of developers and management toward testing (once again, mindset). Developers must be expected to do everything in their power to prevent defects and to catch them before the software reaches QA and customers. It should be a point of pride that customers do not encounter defects and that defects found by QA are fixed as rapidly as possible. This does not mean that developers spend the bulk of their time doing manual testing, but it does mean that developers need to look at the task of software development as more than just writing code. The practices in this chapter are intended to help build a defect prevention culture, which is an important part of developing a professional attitude to software development.

The Role of Quality Assurance

Emphasizing defect prevention does not eliminate the need for a QA organization. Rather, the role of Quality Assurance is completely different than it is in a predominantly defect detection oriented culture. Good QA people are paranoid about ensuring the quality of the product before it reaches customers and are conscientious about their job. The role of QA *should* be to ensure that new features work in ways that customers expect them to and that the product as a whole is capable of meeting customer's needs.

In a culture that emphasizes defect detection, QA's actual ability to fulfill its role is significantly impacted by technical debt in the product. As technical debt accumulates, QA will spend an ever-increasing amount of time regression testing, because as new features are added, previously present features will break, and the product overall will begin to behave in unpredictable ways. Regression testing often consists of mindless *sweeps* through the product where each feature, button, or menu item is tested. Regression testing is not realistic because it does not represent how customers use the product; it is too low-level. Hence, real customer problems are rarely found through mindless regression testing. In addition, because the QA team is tasked with managing large numbers of defects, team members will spend an increasing amount of their time prioritizing and sorting defects, and this will detract from the time they have available for testing.

The end result of QA's spending too much time on low-level testing and being relied upon too much for defect detection is that defects in new features and serious workflow problems are going to be shipped to and found by customers. As shown in Figure 5-2, this is *the* most expensive scenario for fixing these problems because of the time delay between when the defect is introduced and fixed. Unfortunately, the cost of defects is a hidden cost in software organizations because defects are accepted as part of the process,

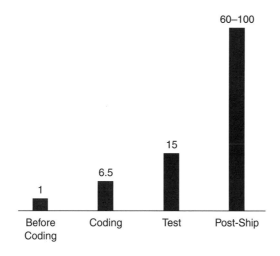

Figure 5-2
The relative cost of fixing a defect increases the greater the time between when the defect was first introduced and when it is fixed. The most expensive scenario is when a defect is found at a customer site and then requires fixing [Pressman 1992].

so it is virtually impossible to calculate the true cost of defects, though some have tried [Rothman 2000]. However, it should be easy to agree that:

- The cost of fixing a defect can't possibly *decrease*. Few developers are able to return to a section of code without taking extra time to understand the code and the problem again.
- Defects found by customers are the most expensive because of the extra costs of support, problem reporting and tracking, and the need to create and test patches, among other things.

Because of the demands placed on the QA team in a defect detection culture, there is either a constant inability to proactively test new features and workflows, or there is a constant demand to increase the size of the QA team to deal with the load. Unfortunately, neither solution is sustainable.

In a culture that emphasizes defection prevention, QA is able to concentrate on what is important: the fitness of new features and the overall product. In this case, far fewer defects are shipped in the product to customers. The only way to enable a QA organization to focus on what is important is for developers to proactively embrace defect prevention practices.

PRACTICE 1: Ruthless Testing

Ruthless testing is all about developers doing absolutely everything in their power to ensure that their software is as heavily tested as it can be before the software reaches people, both QA and customers.

Ruthless testing is one of the most crucial practices of sustainable development and if there is one practice to focus on, this is it. Ruthless testing is primarily about automated testing. Developers should *not* do any of the following:

- Spend the bulk of their time testing features the way QA or users would.
- Turn themselves into mindless *button pushers* in the hopes of finding problems.
- Spend time writing testing plans or testing scripts (i.e., push this button, then do that) that they or someone else would use to test a

feature. This should remind readers of the need for minimal documentation and practicing the art of doing only those tasks that are of high value. Test scripts may be useful in a QA organization to document tests but they have limited usefulness to developers.

- Advocate the hiring of lower paid workers such as co-ops or interns to perform testing tasks.

All of the above would be a waste of time, effort, and money.

Developers have access to a testing resource that is excellent at repeatedly performing mind-numbingly dull tasks: a computer! Tests can be written as code, keeping the task of software development as a coding exercise with more code produced to complete a feature, but usually more code dedicated to testing than to implementing the feature. Developers still have to do some user-level testing, just as they do today. The difference is that as developers add and change functionality and fix defects, they put in place safeguards in the form of automated tests. These automated tests are then run as often as possible to give the developers confidence that their product is behaving as expected and keeping the expected behavior over time.

There are multiple types, or levels, of testing that can (and should) be utilized in Ruthless Testing as shown in Figure 5-3. Each of these types has varying degrees of effectiveness, which is described in more detail in the following sections.

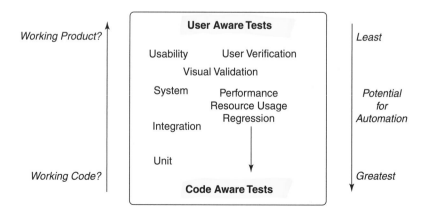

Figure 5-3
The different types, or levels, of tests that should be utilized in ruthless testing. The types of tests are organized by how aware they are of user tasks and code implementation. User-awareness indicates how close the tests are to replicating exact tasks that users perform. Code-awareness indicates the degree of knowledge the tests have with the actual implementation of the product.

Test automation is a critical part of ruthless testing. Code-aware tests have the greatest potential for automation and provide the greatest return for the least amount of effort. The user aware tests of usability, user verification, and visual validation are rarely automated because each of these tests requires human effort for the design of the tests and careful observation and analysis of the test results. However, while code-aware tests can determine whether the code is working as expected, they do not necessarily ensure that the product works as users expect. Hence, ruthless testing requires a strategy that mixes both code-level *and* user-level tests.

Unit Tests: Test-Driven Development

Unit tests are the lowest level of tests you can create for software because they are written with explicit knowledge of the software's classes, methods, and functions. They essentially consist of calling methods or functions to ensure that the results are as intended. Test-driven development means writing the unit tests for new code *before* writing the code and then ensuring that the tests always pass whenever new changes are made [Astels 2003] [Beck 2002a] [Husted and Massol 2003] [Link and Frolich 2003]. In test-driven development, tests are run every time the developer builds the software. The result of the build is either a green light (all tests passed) or a red light (a test failed).

Test-driven development is a powerful way to develop software. It should **not** be viewed as optional, and it is a crucial part of achieving sustainability. Some of the benefits of test-driven development are:

- Code with tests can be modified and refactored with a great deal of confidence because errors are detected immediately by the tests. This is important not only for the developer who originally wrote the code, but also for developers unfamiliar with the code.
- The tests act as invaluable documentation of the behavior of the software. If a change is made to one section of code that changes the behavior expected by another section of code, then the tests will fail. This is vital to preventing defects in existing features.
- Developers who are very good at test-first development report that they spend significantly less time debugging their software; some even report *zero* debugging time!

TIP   Use Mock Objects!

If you deal with databases, network interfaces, user interfaces, or external applications you should learn about Mock Objects [Thomas and Hunt 2002] [http://www.mockobjects.com]. Mock objects are essentially a design and testing technique that let you simulate an interface so that you can test your code in isolation while having control over the types of events and errors that reach your code.

TIP   Be Creative When Implementing Automated Testing.

Automated tests shouldn't always mean manually specifying calls and expected return values and error conditions as in JUnit. In many cases, it is possible to write a program to generate tests for you. For example, suppose you have a piece of software (a method, class, or component) that accepts a string of flags just like the typical UNIX utility (e.g., grep, awk, sed). You could write a program that called the code with the flags in all possible orders. This type of test is extremely thorough and bound to pay off. I have seen cases where libraries that have been in use for years with no tests have tests added to them in this way and serious problems are uncovered, in some cases fixing problems that had been long outstanding and thought to be unreproducible!

Integration Tests

Integration tests test the interface exposed by a collection of classes that are linked or grouped into a library/module/component. Unlike unit tests, they do not understand the implementation of the library. Hence, integration tests can be a useful mechanism to document and test the expected behavior of a library.

Figure 5-4 illustrates the difference between unit and integration tests. In this example, the unit tests for each class in the library test the class's public and private interfaces, while the library's integration tests only test the collective public interface of the library. Hence, integration tests can be considered optional because they are a subset of the collective unit tests. However, integration tests can still be useful because they are separately

Figure 5-4
Integration tests are different from unit tests. In this example, a library called Omega is made up of three classes. Each class has its own unit tests, and the library has a separate set of integration tests.

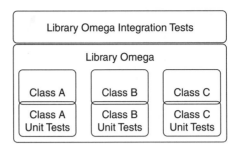

maintained and created from the unit tests, especially if the programmers who depend on the library use the integration tests to document how their code expects the library to behave. The tests don't need to be complete; they only need to test the expected behavior. Two situations where integrations tests are most useful are where a library is used in more than one application (or program) and when a third-party library is used.

One example of when to use integration tests is when you are dealing with a third-party library or any library that the product *imports* in a pre-compiled form. What you need is a test harness and a set of tests that realistically represent how you are using that library, the methods you call, and the behavior you expect when you call those methods. You often don't need to test all the interfaces exposed by the library, just the ones you depend on. Then, as new versions of the library are shipped to you, all you need to do is plug the new version into your test harness and run the tests. The more portions of your software architecture that you can treat as third-party libraries and test in this way, the more robust the interfaces your architecture will have. Having sound interfaces will give you a great deal of flexibility in the future so that at any time you could choose to replace an implementation of one of these interfaces without disrupting the entire system. This is a huge benefit and speaks to the need to have well-designed interfaces that are easily tested.

The Importance of Automated Testing

I first learned the vital importance of automated testing on a team that I worked on that produced networking software. My team had its own live test network, and every time we made a change to our software, we would push the latest software out to the test network and run a number of tests. Some of the tests were manual ones, but the most effective tests were the automated integration tests. Our automated tests ran 24 hours a day, 7 days a week because we found that sometimes problems would not show up until after a large period of time had elapsed, sometimes days. I can remember many instances where changes that I made looked fine during a review but actually contained subtle flaws that only showed up after a number of hours or days of repeated stress testing.

One particular episode I remember on the effectiveness of automated tests involved a very large software application company, best left un-named. They found what they thought was a fault in our network protocol stacks and escalated it as a stop-ship problem. When we received the report, we were puzzled because we knew our automated tests covered the case in question. After a discussion, we found out that they thought it was our problem because their code worked on our competitor's protocol stacks. They were very stubborn and refused to admit the problem was in their code, so we got a binary of their software, installed it in our test network, and then ran it over the weekend under a special debugger with a trigger for it to stop when the error condition we were looking for occurred. Monday morning we came in, captured the offending assembly code, called them and said, "We don't have your source code, but you should be able to find it at the given address and reproduce it using our test suite." We sent them the test suite, and they found that the problem actually did occur on the other operating systems but with different symptoms. Then they found that users *had* reported the problem to them, but they had never been able to reproduce it!

System Tests

System tests are automated tests that cover the functioning of the complete, integrated system or product. System tests know nothing about the structure of the software, only about what the product is intended to do from the user's standpoint. System tests are intended to mimic the actions a user will take, such as mouse movements and keyboard input, so that these inputs can be fed into the application in the desired order and with the desired timing.

System tests are the most difficult type of test to implement *well.* This is because in order to be useful over the long term, the system test capabilities must be designed into the software. Also, it is exceptionally difficult to add system test capabilities to existing software. For new software, the extra design effort is worth it since well-thought-out system tests can be extremely effective and can significantly contribute to the productivity of the development team by reducing the dependence on people to manually test the software and also by providing an additional mechanism to prevent defects reaching people (i.e., QA and customers).

Design testability into your product. Too many teams rely on external test harnesses or manual testing by people and learn to regret not investing the extra effort. The complexities of modern computer applications make it difficult to create automated system tests. Modern applications contain complexities such as multiple threads of execution, clients and servers that exchange unsynchronized data, multiple input devices, and user interfaces with hundreds of interface elements. The result is highly nondeterministic behavior that, without built-in testability, will lead to unreproducible problems.

Record and Playback

Because of the complexity of automating system-level testing, most software organizations choose to leave system testing to its QA organization (i.e., people). However, this is a wasted opportunity because most software products, especially new ones, could greatly benefit from a *record and playback* architecture.

Many applications have a built-in logging capability. As the application runs, it records the actions it is taking in a log file. Log files can be useful when debugging a problem. In most cases, however, logging is only intended for the programmers. Imagine if it were possible to read the log file back *into* the application and have the application perform all the operations recorded in the log file in the same sequence and at the same time to produce the same result as when the recording was made. That is record and playback. With such architecture, recreating problems and debugging them becomes almost trivial [Ronsse et al 2003].

Record and playback is equally effective in deterministic and nondeterministic applications[1]. One example of a highly nondeterministic application where record/playback is widely employed is in the computer gaming industry. In computer games, game companies invest a great deal of effort in creating special-purpose game engines. These engines take the game terrain, levels, characters, props, etc. and render them in real-time in response to the inputs of one or more users. Game engines are complex pieces of software that must consider multiple inputs (such as in a multiplayer game) where characters in the game can interact with each other and the contents of the scene, and these interactions have a notion of time, space, and sequence; interactions are different depending on where a character is relative to other characters at any given time. Because of these complexities, many game companies have by necessity designed record/playback into their game engines so they can quickly diagnose problems that without record/playback would be virtually impossible to reproduce and fix. In some 3D game engines the playback even allows the use of a completely different camera viewpoint, which is like being a neutral third-party observer to the game play. Many useful articles can be found written about these game engines on game developer web sites such as http://www.gamasutra.com.

The Automation of User Interface Testing

One of the most frequently cited complexities in system testing is testing a product's user interface. One way to test applications with any type of user interface is through a record and playback architecture where all user input is captured in the recording and can be played back (another is to use mock objects, which are described above). With a well-structured application, this might allow the tests to be run in batch mode without the user interface, though this is not necessarily required. However, even if you don't have a record and playback architecture, there are still some useful tests that can be automated.

---

1. Deterministic programs are those where there is a single line of execution that, when provided with some inputs, will always produce the same output. Nondeterministic programs have multiple execution paths that interact with each other in a complex way depending on some time-based inputs.

It is possible to use unit/integration tests on the application logic "underneath" the user interface. In this case, the most effective way to test is to start by separating the application logic from the implementation of the user interface [Astels 2003], such as through use of the Model-View-Controller pattern [Gamma et al 1995]. In terms of testing, given this type of separation of logic, it is very easy to implement unit and integration tests for the non-UI parts of the software. Manual testing of the UI will still be needed, but this would be visual validation testing. The more extensively the underlying application logic is tested, the more the visual validation can focus on the unique aspects of the user interface, such as ensuring that UI elements are displayed correctly.

Visual Validation Testing

Visual applications (those that produce an image, movie, or allow the user to interact with their data in real time) are the most complex to produce automated tests for. There are many cases where a person must look at the visual output or interact with the program in some way (such as in a computer game) to ensure that the application actually produces the outputs that it should. For example, in a 2D graphics application, the only feasible way to ensure that a circle created by the program, especially if it is anti-aliased[2], is really a circle, is to look at it.

It is important to ensure that the amount of visual verification required is at an optimal minimal level. This is only possible by automating the code-aware tests as much as possible to ensure that focus can be put on the verification, not say testing for regressions. This can be restated as: ***Use time spent testing by people wisely; don't get people to do tests that a computer could do.***

It should be noted that some aspects of visual validation could also be automated. If the visual output can be captured as images, a database of correct images (as determined by a person) can be used to ensure that images created with the new version of software are the same as the correct images, or different because they should be.

---

2. Anti-aliasing uses shading to create the appearance of a smooth line on the screen.

Don't Forget about the Economics of Automated Testing

Remember that it costs time (and money) to write automated tests. Some people claim that writing an automated test the first time costs between 3 and 30 times more than running a test manually. Hence, don't try to automate everything, especially if it involves building up a large infrastructure outside of the actual code that makes up your product and is used by customers. Concentrate on tests that have the highest value or the highest costs to run manually. And if you can, build testability into your software.

Performance Testing

Every piece of software should have some performance goals. Performance tests ensure that your application achieves or exceeds the desired performance characteristics. Performance could be measured in one or all of unit (e.g., to test the performance of frequently called methods or functions), integration, or system tests. The most common way to do performance testing is by using system timers in your tests and either logging the results so they can be compared or graphed against previous test runs or by creating a test failure if the performance is not within some expected range. Alternatively, there are quite a few commercial and open source performance testing applications available. My current favorite is *Shark*, which is a tool available from Apple for development on OS X.

Run-Time Monitoring

Software should be built with testability in mind. One useful but underutilized idea is to build in run-time monitors. A run-time monitor is a piece of code that can be enabled or disabled and displays or saves a log of critical events (e.g., messages, input/output, memory usage). Run-time monitors augment automated tests, because sometimes it is useful to get live data while the application is running (even at a customer site).

> In my experience, it's best to carefully choose a small number of useful monitors that are chosen for the application area. For example, if you are concerned with real-time performance, then a useful monitor would be one that does simple run-time performance analysis and timing so that performance problems can be isolated quickly.

Resource-Usage Testing

Resource usage testing ensures that your application is using desirable amounts of memory, CPU, time, disk bandwidth, network bandwidth, for example. Resource usage tests can be valuable to catch problems early and without a person having to explicitly monitor them. Each project will have its own set of resources that are more important to monitor than others. Some of the factors are:

- *The type of application.* A web-based application uses completely different resources than a desktop application. They might both use a database, but the desktop application is going to use native operating system resources, while the web-based application is going to use resources on the web server and network bandwidth to the client.
- *The operating system.* Each operating system has its own set of resources that are available to applications. For example, in Microsoft Windows it is important to pay attention to graphics contexts because if they are *leaked* by the application, the application may crash when it tries to create a new graphics context when no more are available.
- *The programming language.* Languages such as C and C++ are notorious for ensuring that programmers must carefully manage their memory allocations. If they don't, *memory leaks* may result (memory leaks are described in detail below).

Regression Testing

Regression tests are tests written to prevent existing features or bug fixes from being broken when new code changes are made. They aren't a different kind of test, because these tests should be built into unit, integration, and system tests. However, they are included as a reminder: Be sure to add tests when you fix a defect—there is nothing more frustrating than fixing a defect more than once!

Usability Testing

Usability testing is different from all the other types of testing already discussed because it cannot be automated. However, for any application with a user interface, usability testing is a critical part of sustainable development and should *not* be considered optional unless the interface is brain-dead simple, and even then I'd still recommend it.

Usability testing involves observing real users in realistic conditions using the product in a controlled environment. In a usability test [Rubin 1994] [Dumas and Redish 1999], careful attention must be made to not guide or bias users. Users are asked to perform a predefined task and think out loud while they use the system with more than one person observing and taking notes. The reason several people should observe the tests is to ensure there is no bias or ability to ignore issues that arose. When done well, usability testing will quickly uncover interface and interaction flaws that won't normally be uncovered until after the product ships. Hence, doing usability testing as early as possible is definitely a flavor of being ruthless.

Usability Testing Is Humbling!

I can think of a number of occasions where I have observed a usability test of a feature I implemented. As an observer in these tests, it is very tempting to just jump up and demonstrate the "correct" way to use the feature, but that would defeat the purpose of the testing! As a programmer, it is easy to understand a feature and how to use it. However, I have seen very few cases where a feature can be deemed usable without some form of alteration.

User Verification Testing

User verification testing is typically the last type of testing that is performed before a product is installed and actually used by customers. It isn't necessary for all products and will depend on the customer. For example, government agencies often demand verification testing, as do customers who use products where a product failure could result in the loss of a life, injury, or damage. This testing involves real users performing real work on the software in conditions that are as close as possible to how the end-users will use the product, often in parallel with the live system. In applications such as mission-critical software, this testing could take weeks to months due to the high cost of failure after the software is installed.

Large Customers Need Automated Tests, Too

I was fortunate to work with a customer a number of years ago that did thorough verification testing before installing any new piece of software. This customer was a large insurance firm with a complex computing environment. I think the company was visionary in its use of automated testing, because it developed a comprehensive suite of tests and a separate test environment on an isolated network. Before the company installed any software in its main network, it would install it on its test network and run its automated tests for as many hours (or days) as it felt was necessary.

I enjoyed working with this customer because this company always gave my team prompt feedback on problems it found with our product. Every time the company found a failure, we made sure that our tests were modified to prevent the same problem from occurring again. This led to an excellent working relationship. Because our automated test suite caught problems before they reached this customer and we had a proven ability to respond, this customer was not interested in working with anyone else.

Resources Required for Ruthless Testing

Ruthless testing is only effective if tests are easy to run and results can be obtained and analyzed quickly. Ruthless testing may require additional computing resources and effort, depending on the size and complexity of the product. Extra investment is required when it is impossible for the team to quickly and easily run and analyze tests on its own. You may need to also invest in some centralized or shared fast computers, although an investment in distributed testing might be advisable, where spare CPU cycles are used to run tests, especially at night. Where many tests are being run, some custom programs might help to simplify the presentation and analysis of results.

What If You Can't Implement All the Recommended Types of Tests?

The important thing to remember when considering where to spend your testing investment is that *any* automation is better than none. Everything you do should start with test-driven development because this instills the discipline of testing into the organization. Then, automate as many system-level tests as you can, preferably in the form of record/playback, because this will ensure testing is designed into your software architecture. If you augment these with usability and user verification testing, your project will be in very good shape.

What If You Are Working on a Product That Has No Tests?

Don't use the fact that no tests currently exist as an excuse to not write tests! Any investment in testing is better than none. Start by adding tests for all your new code, in problem areas of your code, and as changes are made to existing code.

What If Your Tests Take Too Long to Run?

For tests such as unit tests where fast turnaround is required, it may be necessary to reduce the number of tests. If you have this problem, please stop to congratulate yourselves before doing anything else—this is a **great** problem to have! To reduce the number of tests, you should consider doing some test coverage analysis to identify your *cornerstone tests*. Cornerstone tests are tests that provide the maximum benefit (i.e., coverage) with the minimum of overlap with other tests. You could use the cornerstone tests to reduce the number of tests by removing those that provide overlapping coverage.

PRACTICE 2: Use Available Tools

A large number of tools are available to software developers that can help with defect prevention. Some of the available tools offer easily automated ways of detecting common coding errors. Other tools help a team communicate better through offering automated ways to document code and code structure; better communication helps prevent defects by making it easier for the team to understand code and its structure before attempting to change or enhance it.

There are some obvious tools, and some that aren't as obvious, as outlined in the following paragraphs. In most cases, these tools are very easy to set up and use, and many can be integrated into your product build for maximum effectiveness.

Teams that take the time to find the right tools for their projects and then integrate them into their daily workflow are definitely on the right track when it comes to defect prevention. Better tools are becoming available all the time, and it is important for a team to know what tools are available and how they could help.

Compiler

A *compiler* is the perfect example of a tool that virtually everyone uses, but that is not always as effectively as it could be. Compilers are really good at detecting common coding problems. Unfortunately, some potentially serious problems actually show up as warnings, and the problem with warnings is that they are too easy to ignore. You should understand the warnings that your compiler produces, prioritize the warnings, and, if at all possible, turn many of the warnings into *errors*. Then, make sure your code compiles without the warnings you care about. The extra flags won't add to your compile time; even if all the compiler does is catch what would have been a defect once a month, it's still worth the effort. That's one defect a month that is caught before your product reaches QA and your customers.

Source Code Analyzer

A source code analyzer is a tool that detects common coding errors that require more sophisticated analysis than that performed by a compiler. These tools are obviously language dependent and typically come with a default set of errors they look for, but they can also be customized so you can ignore certain errors or even add your own rules. Here is a very short list of common problems that a source code analyzer could catch for you.

- If you are using exception handling, it's almost always a bad idea to have an empty catch block, since it means that if the exception does occur, you have no control over how it is dealt with.
- Code that has probably been copied and pasted. It's obviously impossible to perform an exhaustive search for all duplicated code, but duplicated code is always bad because it means that bugs in the duplicated code need to be fixed in more than one place; what should be a single defect and fix almost always turns into many.
- Short global variable names. Global variables are rarely desirable, but if you have to use them, they should at least have meaningful names . . .!
- Switch statements that don't have a default case.
- Deeply nested if statements and method complexity. Complexity is usually a measure of how much nesting there is of statements.
- An object's constructor method calling a virtual method. The problem in this case is that the object could be partially initialized when the method is called, which could lead to an unknown state.

Source code analysis tools are a pretty recent development. One of the better tools that I have used is PMD for Java. PMD is open source (http://pmd.sourceforge.net) and requires less than a day to set up; most of the work involves turning off checking for undesirable rules. I sincerely hope that more open source projects are started to cover other common programming languages and development platforms and APIs, since every language and API has good and bad uses.

If you are not using Java, PMD also comes with a tool called CPD (copy-paste code detector). CPD works with Java, C++, and C and is well worth looking into because it is surprisingly good at finding code that has been simply copied and pasted. Copying and pasting code is a lazy shortcut that developers often resort to when they are, for example, creating a new class with a method almost identical to an already existing class. Copying code is never a good thing because if there is a bug in the copied code, invariably the bug will get fixed in only one place. CPD will help ensure code that should obviously have been refactored in the first place never makes it into the product code.

Test Coverage Analysis

A tool you should consider using is one that measures how many source code statements are "covered" by your tests. This measure of coverage can be used to help add tests to get more coverage and even to remove tests, which can be necessary when your tests take too long to run.

Test Coverage: Handle with Care!

Test coverage is an aid to your testing efforts and should never be a focal point. It is a metric that is most useful to ensure all areas of the code receive at least some desired level of testing coverage. Beyond that, the value is dubious in my experience.

A development team at a large well-known software company decided a few years ago to focus on achieving 100 percent code coverage in its tests. They actually did it, but found that their product was unreliable and unstable. The reason? In order to achieve the 100 percent coverage, the developers removed error checking for boundary conditions!

Execution Profiler

An execution profiler is a tool that helps pinpoint performance problems in code. Typically, these tools give you a report of the methods/procedures/functions in your code that are taking the most time in a given run. You can use these reports to examine the methods in question and determine if there are any obvious performance issues.

DEFECT PREVENTION

Execution profilers are often available in an IDE or as commercial tools or open source software. Examples of excellent commercial tools are VTune from Intel and Shark from Apple.

Event Logging

Event logging is a diagnostic tool that lets you put "print" statements in your code to record a log of execution. Instead of writing your own, pick up an open source logger, if you can, such as log4j (Java) or log4cplus (C++).

Source Code Documentation

Source code documentation tools typically extract documentation from your source code and generate a set of web pages. Some tools also produce class hierarchy diagrams and searchable indexes that let you find method and variable names quickly. Probably the best-known source documentation tool is JavaDocs, which is available as part of the Java language. If you aren't using Java, or need to produce documentation for many languages, there are many open source projects (I recommend doxygen), which you should evaluate before attempting to build your own.

Memory and Resource Leak Detection

Memory leaks result when a developer allocates memory for an object but doesn't free it, and she is using a language and/or run-time environment that has no memory management (such as C and C++). I use the term resource leak to refer to the related case when the developer uses a system resource (such as a graphics context) and stops using it without releasing it back to the system. Both of these types of leaks result in serious defects and unpredictable application behavior that customers definitely notice.

> ### TIP   A Simple Leak Detection Method
> One very simple leak detection method you can use is to redefine the memory and resource allocation and free calls with

your own in your debug build. All your redefined versions need to do is increment or decrement a counter. Then, in your unit tests you could simply run all the tests and then print the value of the counter. If it isn't zero, you've probably got a leak somewhere that you could then track down with a real detection tool.

Luckily, there are good tools available to help detect memory and resource leaks. Some IDEs have basic memory leak detection built in, so all you need to do is turn on a compiler flag, and there are also commercially available tools such as Purify and Boundschecker.

Configuration Management

All assets developed for and used in a project should be stored in a configuration management (CM) tool. Having a versioned copy of all your changes will help prevent defects, because the good tools help the arduous and error-prone task of merging new code in with the existing code, especially when there are multiple developers working on the same piece of code. A good CM tool should allow a team to do basic version control (check-in, check-out, labeling or "stamping" the current version of all files in a product, branching of source trees, etc.) over a network and also provide some form of merging changes together.

The Value of CM

This practice seems completely obvious, but it is surprising how many software teams manage versions of their software simply by taking copies and not using a CM tool.

This example is admittedly extreme, but one of my friends worked at a company where the developers kept copies of their product on their local disk with only occasional attempts to keep their copies in sync with each other. One of the most distressing stories my friend related was when a customer received a new version of the product from one of the developers. The customer found a problem in the product and reported it, but this caused panic because the developer's hard drive had crashed and the backups were incomplete. The development team had to try and piece together source code that was as close as possible to what the customer had installed, largely working from memory of the changes made. They eventually fixed the customer's problem, but what took them weeks should have taken only minutes. The distressing part of the story is that after this crisis, the team continued developing as they had before!

Cost is not an acceptable excuse for neglecting to use a CM tool. There are many good CM tools available free or via open source such as CVS. If you have the money, it is also a good idea to buy hardware for your CM database that provides some form of robustness, especially in case of hard drive failures.

CM tools are extremely easy to set up and use, and a good CM tool will save you a ton of time. There is absolutely no reason to not extensively use a CM tool!

The Promise of Open Source

What if all the software teams in the world contributed to the creation of tools that are meaningful to software developers, especially for defect prevention? Commercial software vendors have by and large done a poor job of creating the tools that software developers require to be more efficient and prevent defects. Further, too many software companies invest effort in the creation of their own internal tools, usually because they have a "tailored" environment (or think they do), but also due to a lack of knowledge of what's available or even an inability to contribute because of legal reasons (the work most developers do during work hours is the property of the company).

Open Source tools like junit (and all its derivatives), pmd, log4j, cvs, bugzilla, and Eclipse all show the potential of open source for creating a more powerful software infrastructure for the industry. There is an awful lot of duplicated effort going into proprietary tools, and if even half of that effort were put into building a set of easy-to-use tools, we would all be better off.

PRACTICE 3: Pair Programming and Code Reviews

An important practice to prevent defects is to ensure that someone else looks at new code before it is checked in. This is true whether it's a bug fix or a part of a feature and regardless of the amount of code changed, even if it's only a single line! The main reasons to have someone else look at new code are to ensure that:

- More than one person understands the code. XP rightly calls this "collective code ownership." If more than one person understands the code, it means that there are many people who understand the overall behavior of the system. This is very important to defect prevention, because any added knowledge in the team of overall system behavior is a good thing and will help everyone on the team think ahead and be able to more accurately predict where future problems might occur or where new changes conflict with or duplicate already existing code.
- Shared code understanding also means that it is easier for team members to pass their knowledge on to someone else, such as new team members. It also prevents people being "locked" into one section of the code or being a single point of failure because they are the only ones who understand it. This is a bad thing; not only for the individual's career but also for the company (what happens when the key person get sick?).
- Ruthless testing is employed. Part of the job of the second person is to think about the tests and ensure that the tests cover all the important cases. In many ways, the reviewer can look at the "fitness" of the solution just by knowing what the user problem is and examining the tests to ensure they meet the desired criteria.
- The new code is not an ugly workaround and does not duplicate any already existing code.
- The new code does not contain any obvious logic errors.

There are two primary ways to ensure someone else looks at code changes: pair programming and code reviews. Unfortunately, most software texts emphasize code reviews, but the optimal approach should actually concentrate on pair programming, with code reviews as an adjunct or outlet.

The primary advantage of a code review is that it gets a number of people together to discuss some code. Learning happens and good ideas are exchanged. However, code reviews are actually very poor at finding logic errors unless an inordinate amount of time is spent in the actual reviews, and this extra time is in my opinion hard to justify unless you are writing software where there is the potential of a catastrophic effect if the software fails (such as a person being killed). The problem with finding logic errors is that the best time to find them is while the code is being written; when presented with a mass of code as in a code review the logic and order behind the creation of the code is no longer evident. Hence, pair programming.

Pair programming is simple. Two programmers work at the same computer on the same problem at the same time with one monitor, keyboard, and computer. Pair programming is much more effective than code reviews at finding logic errors and preventing defects because both programmers will bring their shared *and* differing perspectives to the problem. In fact, all the benefits of having someone else look at code before it is checked in are maximized with pair programming. Additionally, pair programming is an excellent means to introduce new team members to the software by pairing them with a more experienced team member. There is no better way to learn a software system than to help solve real problems in it.

The only problem with pair programming is that it is a very *intense* experience that can be stressful and possibly even demotivating for one or both people in the pair. It isn't for everyone and it shouldn't, in my opinion, be viewed as something that is done exclusively all day, every day, by every member of a software team.

The benefits of pair programming are clear. But what isn't talked about, except by those who use pair programming as an excuse to not use XP or agile development, are some of the drawbacks of pair programming. For the "observer" in the pair, it can be annoying watching someone else type and make the same typing mistakes over (and over) again, type too slowly, jump around too much, and in short not have "control." For the person typing, it can be frustrating to have someone interrupt your train of thought or make suggestions that are on a wildly different line of thinking. More serious drawbacks of pair programming show up when there is a personality conflict in the team. Although these situations are relatively rare, they cannot be ignored because they can be very disruptive to the team.

I think the optimal approach to ensuring that someone else looks at every software change is to use a mix of pair programming and lightweight code reviews. Pair programming should be used as much as possible, but with an available outlet to work independently with joint code reviews when required. The key thing is to keep the code reviews lightweight using some of the following suggestions:

- It is critical to follow the "continuous integration" practice outlined in Chapter 4 on Working Software. Changes should be small and easily described. Don't wait days or weeks or months before having code reviewed, because that will require a great deal of effort to review and minimize the benefits of the review.
- Given small changes for review, exchange them frequently in e-mail or have someone drop by for a quick walkthrough.
- Avoid needless documentation and "ceremony" for the review. Keep it simple enough to ensure that the benefits are gained.
- Buy a projector for your team and hold group review sessions with critical code and its associated tests. Try to keep these fun and focused on benefits such as learning, not on trying to find "mistakes" and "errors." Rely on the tests to find the major errors, so your team can derive the most benefit.

PRACTICE 4: Lightweight Root-Cause Analysis

Use regular lightweight root-cause analysis sessions to understand what caused a defect and how to prevent it in the future. Root-cause analysis is an attempt to understand the real cause of a problem and to prevent similar problems in the future. It's important to stress *lightweight*; the goal is to learn and move on so that you can minimize the number of defects in your product and hence minimize the amount of time spent fixing defects overall.

Make sure your team and your users know the difference between a defect that must be fixed and one that doesn't or probably never will get fixed. You can't afford to let defects hang around because any form of defect backlog, even a short-term one, is a drain on a team's focus and time.

You should also consider having a special *won't fix* state for defects in the following categories:

- The cost to fix the defect far outweighs the benefit to the user. If the user benefit is high, then you should seriously consider rebranding the bug fix as a feature and treat it as such in planning.
- The benefit to the user is very low or questionable.
- The defect only occurs through some bizarre sequence of events that is virtually impossible.

Mark these defects *won't fix* and review the list periodically (perhaps once a year). Make sure that the database entry records your reasoning, and if that reasoning no longer applies, you might want to consider fixing the defect after all.

Well-run root-cause analysis sessions are an extremely efficient mechanism to get a team to collectively understand typical defects in a product and also to build collective ownership for preventing these defects in the future. The goal is to be super efficient time-wise and to understand the answers to three questions:

1. **What caused this defect?** If possible, record the cause of the defect in your defect-tracking database. Hopefully, you can do this update live during the root-cause analysis session itself. The goal is **not** to assign blame; the *only* reason to answer this question is so you can answer the following questions:
2. **What mechanism, had it been in place, would have caught this defect?** This question helps categorize what is required to catch defects before they get to customers. For example, would a test have caught the defect? More user testing? More communication between users and developers? A simple assertion failure in the code?
3. **How can we prevent this defect or this class of defect in the future?** The best possible method to prevent defects from recurring again is to write a test or series of tests and add them to your test suite. Fixing defects is not an optimal use of time, and the greater the amount of time your team spends preventing defects, the more time you'll have to develop the features your customers need.

Of these questions, 3 is the most important. The only reason you answer the first two is so you can answer 3. This is counter to what some consider standard doctrine for root-cause analysis—that the answers to the first two questions are where the effort should be spent. I strongly disagree. The value in root-cause analysis is in preventing other defects and in promoting a shared understanding in the team about what can be done to prevent defects. Quite often there are also useful discussions about what constitutes good code and bad code. By not apportioning blame and focusing on prevention, you are putting the emphasis on the positive aspects of the exercise, in particular the aspects that emphasize team learning and collaboration.

It is important to have a simple and efficient process for the root-cause sessions. This ensures the process is repeatable, easily understood, easily changed, and therefore lightweight. A simple process might be something like:

- Have a computer in the session with your bug tracking system running so changes can be made live during the session.
- The root-cause session is not just for developers. Users and other team members should be present. Even if they get bored during some of the more technical conversations, their presence helps keep everyone motivated to keep those conversations short. Also, most software projects will find that a surprising number of defects would have been prevented through better communication. Having everyone present will help ensure that there is shared recognition of the communication problems so that everyone can work toward communicating more effectively.
- Start by reviewing the priority of all the newly reported defects. Users should have the final say on the priority. Determine which defects are going to be fixed before the next session and assign them. Some defects may not be defects at all but feature requests. Other defects may require major effort to fix and so are effectively features. Convert these to feature cards so they can be prioritized during upcoming iteration planning meetings. Some defects will be fixed later by work that is already underway. These can be kept as a backlog; hopefully, these will be the only defects in your backlog.
- Answer the questions. Remember that the benefit of this exercise is the collaboration and the process, not the documentation of the

results. Therefore, you could keep the documentation simple by categorizing the answers so that you can review them later in a chart.

- Spend a bit of time on your answers to question 3. Are there changes you can make right now to prevent similar problems in the future?
- Have a quick discussion about the key lessons learned from the defects discussed in the session.
- Whenever you do a retrospective, spend some time discussing the data you've collected through root-cause analysis.

TIP   Try to Avoid Setting up Separate Root-Cause Analysis Sessions.

If you keep the number of defects low in your product, try including defects in your iteration planning sessions. Write up index cards for each defect that is obvious to the users. Then you can do the root-cause on each defect's index card or record the information in your bug tracking system. This has the advantage that the defects are prioritized against all the other work that must be done in the iteration and will avoid YAM – yet another meeting.

You should constantly evaluate how often to hold root-cause sessions and the process used in your retrospectives. I have worked on projects where we did it every day, once a week, once a month, and not at all. It all depends on how much time you want to spend at any one time and possibly also on where you are in your project. The key thing is to be agile and to anticipate a need to change the session frequency.

Root-Cause Analysis

Not all the teams I've worked on or with did root-cause analysis. However, as I mentioned in Chapter 4, there was one team where this was one of our cornerstone practices. Every week, my team sat down and went through every single defect in our software. These meetings lasted anywhere from 5 to 30 minutes, depending on the number of new defects we had to discuss. We briefly discussed every defect found in the previous week, and we focused our discussion on how we could prevent this and similar defects in the future, almost always through enhancing our automated or manual test plans.

Our weekly reviews kept us focused on eliminating and preventing defects. Essentially, we were motivated to keep our defect count low so we could maximize the amount of time working on new features and minimize the amount of time required for the weekly review. The weekly reviews also ensured that we fixed new defects in the week following the meeting. This practice allowed us to ship our product over a number of years with large numbers of new features and the same number of defects year after year, even with all the new features.

Of all the practices in this book, root-cause analysis is probably the most prone to being ineffective and a time drain. Hence, it is vital to discuss your root-cause sessions in your retrospectives. Are they as effective as they could be? Is everyone who needs to be there? Are too many people attending? What changes to the process can be made to make them shorter and maximally effective? Talk about them as a team and aim to constantly improve their effectiveness. As with any practice, it is important to see some benefits early or the practice will not stick.

When starting out, I would advise being conservative. For example, if you have any kind of defect backlog, don't even think about doing root-cause analysis on the backlog until you have an efficient process that has been refined through applying it to some or all of your newly reported defects. I learned this the hard way on a project with a backlog of hundreds of defects. I was the new person on the team, so in a fit of enthusiasm, I organized a review session. After an hour, I realized this practice was a non-starter for this team because they had too many defects to cope. Many of the defects had been reported months to years earlier, and it became clear to me that all the team could do was concentrate on the defects that customers complained about the most. I was only on the project for a short time, and unfortunately I know the problem with the backlog was never addressed. The project was cancelled shortly after I left, largely because of the return on investment of the project: it took too many more developers to keep the project going than were justified by the market size.

Summary

Defect prevention is an important principle for sustainable development. Practices must be used to catch defects as early as possible, especially via automated means, so that the burden of testing is not placed on people, whether they are QA, a testing group, or customers. One of the most critical practices for sustainable development, *ruthless testing*, is described in this chapter. Ruthless testing is a challenge to teams to go beyond test-driven development and to build testability into their software. When software has testability built in, then everyone, from developers to QA to customers, benefits. Another critical practice is that of ensuring that someone else looks at your work before it is added to the product. This can either be done via pair programming or code reviews, though pair programming is preferred because problems are caught immediately.

The other principles described in this book reinforce defect prevention. A focus on a working product is important to ensure that the team does not spend all its time fixing broken tests. Likewise, an emphasis on design helps defect prevention because one of the design goals should be building in testability. Also, well-designed software is easier to test because it is well structured with clean interfaces that can be easily identified and tested. Finally, continual refinement supports defect prevention by giving the team a process where it can regularly and frequently review and refine their automated testing coverage and processes.

Chapter 6

Emphasis
on Design

Design matters! Well-designed software is obvious to users and to the programmers who work on it. Well-designed software is useful and easy to use, maintain, extend, and understand. And when competition is intense, design is often the difference between winner and loser.

In order to achieve sustainable software development, software must be designed to support and enhance changeability. This is because agility is possible only with the ability to easily modify and extend the software. Imagine that you are tasked with creating a set of playground equipment. If the equipment you design requires a welding torch and hammer to reconfigure, you are in a ton of trouble if your customer asks for changes to the configuration. On the other hand, if your equipment is designed to be modular and is put together with some bolts and a wrench, you can respond to almost any customer request. Software is unfortunately more complex than playground equipment because it is never left in any one arrangement, it is continually changing and evolving.

In sustainable development, you cannot afford to have a product that has a high cost of change because your inability to easily change your product will dictate a slow pace of development that will leave you in continual catch-up mode. Good design practices are one of your most important tools to help control the cost of change.

Design clearly has a critical role in software development, regardless of the methodology used. Design is also the hardest aspect of software development to get right because of factors such as schedule pressures, the people on the project, and continual change. As a result, designs fall across a spectrum that ranges between being *over*designed and *under*designed, with an unfortunate number of projects at either end.

Overdesigned projects are typically the result of overzealous application of the engineering approach to software development. This is the traditional waterfall top-down design method, which is still the most widely taught approach to software development. Top-down design advocates thorough design before coding, which of course involves understanding requirements before design. This is what most building planners use: They have a stable of mathematics, standard questions to ask the customer, and building codes that help them make the right decisions before they actually begin construction. Unfortunately, when top-down design is applied to software, the result is most often overdesign and a high cost of change. That is, if any software is produced at all—many of these projects turn into exercises that produce stacks of documents but no code.

The other extreme to top-down design is ad-hoc *code-then-fix* development, which is just as bad. In this case, there is little or no design, and change is just as hard because the code is a tangled mess or hard to comprehend. Underdesigned software is painful to work with. It is also unfortunately a great form of job security, because one of the symptoms of underdesigned software is the fact that the code is divided into the exclusive domains of various individuals. These heroes can crank out new features, but heaven help you if they ever leave the project.

In order to achieve sustainable development, you can't rely on top-down or bottom-up development. What is required is a middle ground so you can capture the good points of each: You want to have the discipline and ability to think about good design while at the same time proceeding as rapidly as possible.

Extreme Programming [Beck 2004] outlines *evolutionary* or *emergent* design. This method relies on simple design (only design what you need), refactoring (disciplined code changes), and test-first development (to ensure that the behavior stays as originally intended—see Chapter 5). Evolutionary design works because of a tight feedback loop with end users of the software: The idea is to get the software into their hands as early as possible and then evolve the design as requirements change. However, evolutionary design can lead to unintended oscillation, where the same code is repeatedly changed over and over because sufficient thought was not put into the design:

One of the inherent dangers of any form of iterative development is confusing iteration with oscillation. Good iterative design involves a successive convergence on a workable, adaptable design. Poor iterative design involves flailing around randomly searching for a solution—and mistaking this oscillation for iteration. [Highsmith 2005]

For sustainable development, you need to understand how to balance the good aspects of up-front design and various design techniques with evolutionary design while avoiding the pitfalls of each. With up-front design you need to avoid overdesigning the solution by erring on the side of simple design while at the same time avoiding the documentation trap by focusing on producing software not documents. And you have to avoid design and code oscillation by thinking ahead and having a design vision and guiding principles. The design vision and guiding principles are explained as practices below.

Another way to think about up-front and evolutionary design is through the understanding of good design and good design evolution. Practitioners of up-front design concentrate on understanding what makes a good design, while practitioners of evolutionary design focus on understanding designs that result from evolution and how they evolved:

If you'd like to become a better software designer, studying the evolution of great software designs will be more valuable than studying the great designs themselves. For it is in the evolution that the real wisdom lies. The structures that result from the evolution can help you, but without knowing why they were evolved into a design, you're more likely to misapply them or over-engineer with them on your next project. [Kerievsky 2004]

The reality, however, is that design is hard because you need to understand good design *AND* good design evolution. You can't understand design evolution if you can't recognize good design, and design is pointless without evolution because evolution is inevitable. And good design without evolution is pointless, otherwise the tendency would be to design for the sake of design. Hence, design has a yin (good design) and a yang (good design evolution) and this I think explains why it is so hard to get right. Good design doesn't just happen, it requires hard work and thought plus experience and knowledge. However, I also believe that good design doesn't just emerge from a single individual, no matter how brilliant. Good design requires collaboration, because collaboration provides support as the team collectively works toward their goal while balancing the yin and yang of design.

Design in sustainable software development means creating an environment where decisions are continually made within a framework that emphasizes change and designing for change, while ensuring consistency in the decisions. Design work is recognized as being crucial and something that is done every day by every member of the team in as collaborative a fashion as possible. The challenge is to ensure that the time spent on design tasks is appropriate for what is being designed and that the effort spent documenting the design is appropriate for the conditions of the project and is minimized to the greatest extent possible.

Other elements of design in sustainable software development are:

- *Agile development emphasizes having working software not comprehensive documentation.* In many ways, the agile movement is a reaction to the almost compulsive behavior that requires the production of binder upon binder of design documentation. This type of documentation is rarely kept up to date with the code, and if it is, then the amount of effort required to keep it up to date frequently exceeds or equals the effort required to modify the actual code.
- *Binders of documentation don't solve customer's problems, working products do.* Hence, agile development stresses the working product and lightweight ways of documenting the design work that the team naturally does every day.
- *The requirement for documentation increases with the size and complexity of the project or where there is distributed development.* If you can't get all the developers in one room on a regular basis, then more documentation is required—with the goal, as always, of keeping the documentation as simple as possible.
- *The primary value of design work is the process of doing the design itself, not the documentation of the design.* Documentation increases comprehension and the ability to communicate about the design, but reading design documentation is nowhere near as effective as actually participating in the design process itself.
- *Collaboration and face-to-face communication are a key part of design in agile development.* The challenge is finding the right media to enhance communication and collaboration. For collaborative design

sessions, a discussion around one or more whiteboards in pseudo-UML is often the best approach with the documentation of the discussion being a digital photo that can be posted on a team web page for reference [Ambler and Jeffries 2002].

- *Teams need to discuss and understand their design criteria.* What are the attributes of the design that matter the most? These guiding principles are a critical part of design and help ensure consistent design decisions over time.

- *Agile development advocates simple design.* According to many, this means only designing and coding what is needed immediately. I think this is impractical, because if you *know* you will need something, you should go ahead and design it and build some or all of it. The key, of course, is knowing what you absolutely need and what you might need. This is why design must be collaborative; you shouldn't make these decisions by yourself. Use the wisdom of your team.

- *Teams must design for change.* The constantly evolving complex ecosystem of technologies, markets, and competition that software systems inhabit means that the design must promote change, particularly in areas of the product where change is most likely. An example might be the use of a third-party component such as a web browser or instant messaging system. Users may already have their own solutions and will resist your product if you install a solution they already have, so a logical design decision would be to spend the extra time to design an abstract interface that will allow the integration of a component of choice. This independence will also provide you the flexibility to change preferred components and deal with new and (up to a point) old versions of the component.

In typical software projects there are many kinds of design. The most prevalent are the design of the software architecture (classes, hierarchies, methods, etc.), the user interface, web site, marketing and sales material, user documentation, test infrastructure, and database structure. I am intrigued by the idea that while each of these areas is different, there are common elements that can be applied. Hence, although this chapter focuses on software design, the design practices are applicable to other areas of design as well.

PRACTICE 1: Design Vision

From a project management standpoint, iterative development is really hard if you don't have a vision. Hence, just as you need a vision for the project as a whole, you should have a vision for your design as well, even if all you are doing is adding to an already existing code base. A design vision, or conceptual design, is an overall picture of the pieces of your software: what they are, what each does, and how they interoperate to solve the task at hand. Without a design vision, oscillation will likely result because the team will not have a clear idea of how the software is and should be structured.

The design vision can be a simple hand-drawn annotated sketch on a whiteboard or a UML diagram. My personal bias is toward a hand-drawn UML diagram on a whiteboard that is kept up to date. However, it doesn't matter what form the design vision is captured in, as long as it exists.

PRACTICE 2: Guiding Principles

Guiding principles are a short list of statements that specify overall design goals and requirements. Their intent is not to specify the design but to help team members make daily design decisions that are consistent with the design intent. Some people also refer to them as *pillars* because they never change, or are not changed in major ways. They are literally the ideas that everything is built upon.

Guiding principles can be thought of as the vision for the design. However, where the vision describes *what* the project is about, the guiding principles describe *how* the project should be built. As with the vision, the guiding principles need to be understood and agreed to by everyone on the team, and they should be created before the start of the project. Ideally, they should be placed in a visible place where everyone can see them and even pinned up at everyone's desk.

Two important and distinct guiding principles are recommended (others are possible):

- **Engineering guiding principles.** These describe how the project is implemented in technical terms that the project team's developers can understand.

- **User experience guiding principles.** These describe attributes that the user cares about. They are described in a user-centric way that everyone on the team can understand.

The easiest way to explain guiding principles is by example. Let's use one hypothetical example and one real example.

A Hypothetical Example of Guiding Principles

Suppose an IT project team is faced with the task of having to replace an existing backend system for sales tracking. The existing system has an obscure user interface because it has evolved over many years and users complain that they cannot get the information they need without calling for assistance. The system also needs replacing because it is becoming increasingly hard to maintain. And most important, the system needs to be replaced because it can't handle multibyte characters in the customer name field, yet the company has a growing customer base in China and Japan. The new system must be able to store and display Asian characters.

The vision of this project might be something like:

Enable the growth of the company's sales in Asia by providing a sales tracking system that can record and display customer information regardless of geography.

The engineering guiding principles might be:

- Internationalized by default; allow use of any language
- Clean 3-tier architecture
- Replaceable user interface tier
- No hacks or ugly workarounds

Of these guiding principles, you should particularly note words and phrases like "clean 3-tier" and "replaceable." These statements will help ensure that the team is not just groping in the dark toward an end system, but has clear design goals. Even though the team does not have the detailed design at the beginning of the project, these goals will guide team members through every design decision made while the project is developed and help ensure that the end architecture has the desired characteristics. The last guiding principle is a statement that will make the developers think: They should avoid cutting corners and take the time to do things right.

The user experience guiding principles might be:

- Simple: Users of the existing system must be able to use the new system in less than 5 minutes
- Users can generate their own reports with a few minutes of up-front training and no ongoing support
- No glitches when the existing system is replaced

These statements are tangible and measurable and can be used by the product team to make daily decisions. Each of these principles stresses the importance of a clean transition to the new system in a different way. Their presence will help the team with their daily design work by focusing on usability issues that will ease the transition to the new system.

The vision provides the team with a clear statement of what they are building and why. The guiding principles tell the team *how* the product should be built, with the user experience guiding principles describing what the user's experience should be like, and the engineering guiding principles describing the "internal" characteristics of the implementation. In this case, the guiding principles describe the important characteristics of the new system that are required to address the deficiencies of the existing system (which is hard to use, learn, extend, and maintain).

A Real-World Example of Guiding Principles

Adobe's Eve (http://opensource.adobe.com) provides an interesting real-world example of guiding principles. Eve consists of a language that is used to specify user interfaces and a cross-platform layout engine. Although the authors do not use the term guiding principles, they do refer to the goals and requirements of the project:

Goals:
1. Make it easier to specify and modify the layout of a human interface.
2. Have a single definition of the interface for all platforms.
3. Have a single definition of the interface for all languages.

Requirements:
1. Must allow piecemeal incorporation into an application, freeing the entire human interface from being converted in one pass.
2. Generate layouts as good or better than those generated by hand.

These goals and requirements are guiding principles. They were developed before any code was written and therefore serve as the design vision. They are simple statements that serve as daily reminders for the development team as they make design decisions and tradeoffs. For example, the first requirement ensures that the team creates an architecture that allows existing applications to be converted to using Eve piecemeal. This must have been a challenge to the developers because it implicitly dictates that Eve be efficient and as lightweight as possible so that an application being converted does not dramatically increase in size or decrease in speed.

PRACTICE 3: Simple Design

Simple design means you should only design and code what you *know* you need while always striving for simplicity. In the pure definition of simple design (such as in Extreme Programming) the goal would be to only design what you need *immediately*. The problem with this purist approach is that it can lead to oscillation, where a body of code is continually refactored to meet the current requirements because there was no design or planning ahead. If you *know* that something is going to be required, then you should design it and build it even if this means the user may only see a limited immediate benefit. But you need to keep the design as simple as possible. Add the interfaces later that you don't immediately need, for example. Likewise, if a problem is understood well enough to know that its solution can be found in a design pattern, then the pattern should be used because patterns work and are well understood. But patterns aren't perfect (see the Design Pattern practice below), and again you need to always think about simplicity first.

Simple Design and a Hotkey Manager

Simple design, when taken in its pure form (design only what you need immediately), can be a dangerous practice. I observed a project where a number of features required a hotkey manager that mapped a user-defined keyboard hotkey sequence into an application command. Unfortunately, the first two developers who added commands that had hotkeys associated with them did it by hardcoding the hotkeys. Their code worked, but a third developer had to add a new command and realized that the first two simple hotkey implementations conflicted with the changes they needed to make. The result was a major and messy unplanned refactoring exercise that set the project back.

Everyone on this team recognized they needed a hotkey manager. Some simple upfront design work could have made the *total* amount of work much less. Admittedly, the addition of the first hotkey-based command would have been harder because the architecture would have to have been built before the feature. But this work could have been scheduled as an explicit feature (it's good to have visibility in the team that architecture work is being done), and it would have made the addition of all subsequent commands trivial.

Scanning ahead is required. Think about evolving a simple but solid hotkey manager over time, not trying to design the ultimate hotkey manager immediately. This gives you the most amount of flexibility with minimal effort.

TIP   *Making architecture work visible to users.*

In agile development, it is sometimes hard to get architecture work recognized. The cards are user-centric features, as they should be, and users can too easily dismiss architecture work if it doesn't have a recognized benefit.

One effective way I've seen to deal with this problem is to attach architecture cards to user feature cards. The architecture cards not only document what architecture and design work needs to be put in place in order to enable the user feature, but they also document the *benefits* (from a user's perspective) of the work.

In the hotkey case above, a benefit of having a well-designed hotkey manager would be that it makes the addition of subsequent commands trivial. If the users can't see or understand a benefit to architecture work, then perhaps the work isn't necessary after all . . .

Some readers may be uncomfortable with the gray area surrounding being certain that supporting architecture and future extensibility are required. I think it's important to accept that you're going to get it wrong sometimes and over- or underdesign in some instances. That's software development. Fix the problem as soon as you can, learn from the experience, and move on. Teamwork, knowledge, experience, and collaboration are vital to make the right decision. The more people make design decisions with others and use each other as sounding boards for ideas, and the more people learn from each other, and the greater the *collective* experience and knowledge in the team, the greater the chance that the correct decisions are going to be reached.

PRACTICE 4: Refactoring

Refactoring is the process of changing a software system in such a way that it does not alter the external behavior of the code yet improves its internal structure. It is a disciplined way to clean up code that minimizes the chances of introducing bugs. In essence when you refactor you are improving the design of the code after it has been written. [Fowler 1999]

Refactoring involves changing software in a disciplined way so that the structure of the code is changed but the code's behavior remains unchanged. Refactoring is distinguished from merely rewriting code (which developers do all the time) by the discipline required. Refactoring is performed in a disciplined, step-by-step manner with tests in place to catch problems as you proceed. Rewriting is performed in a more ad-hoc delete/replace manner. Refactoring will help keep your code clean; rewriting may not.

We Need the Vocabulary and Discipline of Refactoring

Over the last few years the term refactoring has entered the common vernacular of software developers and managers. However, I am concerned that the term is now *too* commonly used because I don't see enough people doing true disciplined refactoring. What has me concerned is that too many people are confusing generic code cleanups (rewriting) with refactoring. We are losing the value of the *vocabulary* and the *discipline* of refactoring.

Recently in a job interview, the person I was interviewing mentioned that he was being taught refactoring in a university course. When I asked which refactoring methods he used, he looked at me like I had two heads. After a bit of discussion, it turns out the course did not expose the students to any of the refactoring terminology and patterns such as *Extract Method, Extract Superclass,* etc. Hence, the instructor was using the term refactoring in a generic way that had no meaning. And even worse, the students were "refactoring" without having any automated tests! To the students in this course, and to many others in the industry, *refactor* has become a synonym for *rewrite*.

But we need the vocabulary of refactoring! Having a developer tell me she refactored the code is as descriptive as her telling me she had an amazing lunch. However, if a developer tells me he extracted a superclass from a number of classes, I can immediately form an image in my head of what the new class structure is and what the common behavior must be like. I could then apply this knowledge when I look at the code later. Similarly, if she describes her lunch as an eggplant, yellow and red pepper, and portobello mushroom sandwich with a salad on the side, I can get hungry thinking about it.

And we need the discipline of refactoring! Randomly rewriting code does not mean that the code is easier to understand or that the design that results is better. The result could be a mess, and it could lead to oscillation, as the same code is continually rewritten and "cleaned up." Refactoring, on the other hand, should lead to better design because of the steps involved, with automated tests in place to catch problems as the refactoring proceeds and to ensure that the behavior of the resulting changes is correct.

The vocabulary of refactoring provides the power to clearly describe what we mean. The discipline of refactoring helps us avoid random code rewrites that lead to bad code and incomprehensible designs. Let's not lose the value of the vocabulary and discipline and challenge each other to refactor, not rewrite!

The quality of communication is higher with refactoring than with rewriting. This is because with refactoring the person who made the changes can describe the changes through the type of refactoring that was performed. For example, a developer could say "In this change I did an 'extract method' refactoring, removing largely duplicated code from methods X, Y, and Z." The type of refactoring (extract method) immediately conveys to any other developer an immediate and rough feeling of the changes that were made and the complexity of the work required without having to look at the code. Without the refactoring discipline, then, the only recourse for other developers to understand the complexity of the change is to actually look at the code before and after the changes were made.

The level of confidence is higher with refactoring than with rewriting. This is mostly because of the discipline required; with refactoring you are discouraged from trying to make multiple changes at the same time and rather to make changes in small, safe steps that can each be verified through tests. However, when rewriting code, it is too easy to approach a problem with wild abandon, which often results in a worse state or no improvement.

PRACTICE 5: Design Patterns

Design patterns [Gamma et al 1995] are an invaluable resource for software developers. They are essentially a catalogue of solutions to frequently encountered software development problems. Unfortunately, many developers have never heard of design patterns, and others feel that simple design means they should not use patterns because using a design pattern seems like up-front design. But if you are trying to solve a known problem, why reinvent the wheel? The most common design patterns were not just invented, they were observed by some clever and experienced software developers as solutions that worked time and again in different software projects and over time. Patterns are known to work, they are tested, and they have a known behavior.

The value of design patterns as a common vocabulary should not be underestimated. For example, I was in a design discussion one day with my team. One of my teammates started describing a solution in a message-passing system where a message was passed to a number of classes in turn until one of the classes was able to deal with the message. This design provided the greatest amount of flexibility because it allowed the message-handling classes to change independent of the message sources. There was a lot of confusion within the team about how this would work in detail, until I realized that what was being proposed was the Chain of Responsibility pattern. As soon as I pointed this out, the tone of the conversation completely changed. The confusion disappeared because everyone knew what this pattern did. The discussion then switched to how the pattern could be extended to meet the needs of prioritized messages and other detailed, not philosophical, problems. Hence, our common vocabulary of a design pattern as a higher level concept allowed us to have a productive and focused conversation on solving the real problems.

Design patterns can be abused just like any other practice. But just because they have problems doesn't mean they should be ignored. They are too valuable to be ignored, as long as you understand what can go wrong. The most commonly cited problems with design patterns are:

- *They are often overzealously used.* Many examples can be found on the Internet, in software development papers, or in books of projects where it seems like every line of code cleverly employs some design pattern. The software that results from such projects is often unnecessarily hard to understand and modify due to the complex relationships between classes. These projects have sacrificed the rule of simple design for being clever.
- *Design patterns are often used to solve problems where a much simpler solution is possible.* If you use design patterns a lot, you'll find that they're extremely reliable. They solve problems. However, once you get to the point where you know patterns will work the majority of the time, it's often too easy to think about how a design pattern can be used for *all* problems and forget that sometimes a more ad-hoc solution that involves a small bit of code is even better because it's *simpler*! The mistake in this case is thinking of design patterns before simplicity.

EMPHASIS ON DESIGN

- *There are too many different ways to code a pattern.* Since design patterns only provide an outline for implementation, it is still possible to have implementations of patterns that are too complex.
- The use of design patterns can lead to an unhealthy emphasis on up-front design. I have been on projects where people spent too much time trying to analyze a problem so they could try to identify what design patterns would apply. If you aren't sure, don't use a pattern. Simplicity, as always, should be the primary goal. Chances are, if there is a pattern, there it will emerge. You can always refactor to it later, as in [Kerievsky 2004].
- *If you don't know design patterns, the code can appear to be overly complex.* This really can't be helped except through education. However, it is a very real problem when new developers join a project where patterns are used.

The Expected Behavior of Design Patterns

One of the problems with design patterns is that once you are used to them, you expect a certain behavior. I have been surprised on occasion when I look at some code and think, "Ahh, this is implementing the xx pattern," when in fact it is very close to the pattern but has slightly different behavior.

I have encountered a number of cases where the mistaken identification of a pattern has led to wasted time when trying to find a problem or understand the code. I highly recommend documenting the code with the name of the pattern. Also, ensure that everyone on a team understands patterns.

To be consistent with simple design, you don't need to implement all the interfaces if you don't need them, and the simple knowledge that the code is indeed a pattern means that other developers can quickly add the interfaces they need at a later time with full confidence that the expected behavior of the pattern will not be altered.

In summary, design patterns are valuable and they shouldn't be ignored. They do have problems, but as pointed out in the Simple Design practice, teamwork, experience, knowledge, and collaboration are the best way to minimize the risks in software design while maximizing the potential returns. It also helps to recognize that making mistakes is human and part of software development. Fix your mistakes as quickly as possible, learn from them, and move on.

PRACTICE 6: Frequent Rapid Design Meetings

The rapid design meeting is an important mechanism for a team to ensure it is having frequent design discussions. The output of these meetings is a shared understanding of the design issues and a lightweight artifact such as a picture of a whiteboard diagram. This is a departure from more formal design meeting where the output is a document. The desired output of a rapid design meeting is shared understanding, learning, and collaboration. This is a recognition that the source code and automated tests should be where the design is ultimately documented, supported by the most recent design illustrations, and the emphasis should be on the finished product not the design documentation.

There are two types of design meetings that teams can use: the design discussion and the design review. A *design discussion* is when a number of team members get together to discuss design decisions of any kind. A *design review* is an opportunity for a team to analyze its current architecture and discuss short and long-term changes that need to be made.

Design discussions should happen more frequently than design reviews. Most design discussions are going to be purely ad-hoc, when an issue comes up, a number of people get together to discuss it. If ad-hoc discussions aren't taking place on your project, then you have a serious collaboration problem. You may find it useful to introduce a regularly scheduled (e.g., every Friday from 3–5) design discussion so the team can do a deeper review of one particular area of the design, either what has been completed or what needs to be added. These discussions are rarely a waste of time, because they give the entire team a chance to learn and collaborate.

Design review meetings might be held after every Nth iteration, or they might be added to the agenda in a retrospective. As with a retrospective, the goal of the design review is not to assign blame but to learn and provide a positive future direction for the design. Typically, the design review would consist of answering some basic questions about the product's design as it currently stands, such as:

- What areas of the current design are working well?
- What areas of the current design are not working well and should be refactored or rewritten?
- Are there areas of the code that are too tightly coupled?

- Are there areas of the code that are going to be changed a great deal with upcoming features, but are difficult to understand or are fragile?

The result of answering these questions should be a list of problem areas. The team should prioritize these, record the main benefits to the work, incorporate the important work into upcoming iterations, and ensure the rest are recorded (e.g., in the bug-tracking system) to be completed in an upcoming release. As part of incorporating some of this work in upcoming iterations, a recommended approach is to write up a feature card for the work. Even though the work is not a user feature per se, users need to understand why they are not getting a feature and ideally should understand the work (at a high level) so appropriate tradeoffs can be made. People are always skeptical when they hear this suggestion, but in my experience, users care about the stability of the applications they use and are willing to make these tradeoffs when the benefits can be explained to them.

Note that as part of answering these questions, there are excellent opportunities to learn about *good* design and *bad* design. This is team professional development, and it helps everyone on the team improve his or her craft and become better software professionals. It is also an excellent opportunity for more experienced developers to pass on the knowledge they have acquired through their careers.

> **TIP** **Design sessions and reviews are valuable for more than just software.**
> Many possible areas of design are vital to a typical software project (e.g., database, web site, user interface, customer support, etc.). Think about all the areas of design for your project and ensure you spend adequate time on them, too.

PRACTICE 7: Commitment to Rearchitecture

Refactoring is a powerful discipline, but sometimes it is necessary to completely rearchitect and replace some portion of a product. In many cases, this is the preferred approach since the cost of the replacement will over time be less than trying to *bend* the current architecture in the required direction. Therefore, teams (and their management) need to be committed to understanding when rearchitecture is required and be committed to making it happen. Using the chemical plant analogy from Chapter 1, this work should be looked upon as preventive maintenance [md] e.g., taking your pumps offline for work that helps them last longer.

Some of the common reasons for considering rearchitecture work are:

- A team has just released the first version of a product. Shipping a version one of a product is the most difficult task any team can undertake, because team members are most often learning about the product's ecosystem as they are developing. They are bound to make at least one, and most likely quite a few, design decisions that will ultimately limit long-term sustainability.
- A product was written for a single platform (operating system, database, networking protocol, etc.) and it needs to be ported to a new platform. These ports are an excellent opportunity to introduce greater abstraction to hide the underlying platform-dependent implementations. When done well, this type of abstraction should simplify the application and make it easier to modify in the future.
- There have been changes to the underlying technology such as system apis or third-party libraries that the product depends on. Examples might be new input or display devices, or perhaps new hardware or programming models.
- A single-threaded application needs to be multi-threaded. If the goal is to maximize the usage of multiple processors, single-threaded software most often needs to be rewritten to break up its tasks into separable units of computation. Without this rework, usually the only work that can be done is to optimize loops or small sections of code. This type of optimization will not maximize use of additional processors.
- It is natural that the team will understand the problem domain and ecosystem better over time. Often, the current knowledge can be used to further simplify the product.
- The roadmap for the product has changed and in upcoming releases the architecture is going to have to support originally unanticipated workflows. This case is tricky, since you need to practice simple

EMPHASIS ON DESIGN

design and not build unnecessary architecture, but sometimes there are some simple changes that will make these future changes much easier.

- A section of the code is particularly defect prone, is difficult to modify, and/or excessively coupled to other sections of the architecture.

When considering whether rearchitecture is required, it is vital to remember the underlying tenets of sustainable development. Your product is going to last for a long time—hopefully it will last far longer than you can imagine. Consider the consequences of *not* making the necessary decision when the cost is low (i.e., early in time) versus being *forced* to do even more work in the future. It is vital that the decision to rearchitect or not should be made consciously by the team. The most dangerous scenario is when the need to rearchitect is ignored by the team or not discussed due to time pressures, external factors such as overwhelming customer requests or unrealistic expectations, or a *laissez-faire* attitude. Sustainability is often at stake, and the team must have the discipline, and guts, to confront these issues head-on.

Rearchitecture: The Good, the Bad, and the Ugly

In my experience, the most glaring need for rearchitecture work is just after the completion of the first version of a product. There are many reasons for this, but I think the most common is that development teams, no matter how experienced, are bound to make some tradeoffs and mistakes that will cost them over the long-term. I have strong memories of two projects in particular, one good, and the other bad (and ugly).

The Bad and Ugly

This was a product that was built in every team's worst-case scenario: unrealistic deadlines, milestones that were repeatedly missed, and attempts to bring the project back into schedule by adding more people, getting people to work overtime, etc.

The product had an excellent early design vision that was well modularized. To enforce the modularization of the architecture, the build system had been modified to ensure that dependencies were not

---

introduced between modules that should have none. Unfortunately, the build system was complex enough that a decision was made to have a different build system for nightly builds than the one used by developers. The developer build system did no dependency checking, so developers didn't find out about dependency problems until the nightly build. The result was predictable: The nightly builds were always broken, and because of the number of developers, it was time-consuming to figure out which of the many changes broke the build.

Because this was impacting the development team (they couldn't get a good build without a lot of work), the decision was made to turn off the dependency checking. The system then built correctly every time, and the developers were more productive because they no longer had to worry about dependencies. The product did eventually ship.

Unfortunately, the result was akin to a big bowl of sticky spaghetti, there were dependencies everywhere. Heroic efforts could not undo the damage done through that early decision. Business concerns (i.e., profitability) dictated that the team must decrease in size, which largely limited the cleanup attempts to one or two people. The product continued to grow in complexity, and because of the demands for new features, there wasn't time to fix the architecture. The result was an increasingly brittle product, where a change made in one section of the code would cause a problem in one or more unpredictable places. And because the software had lost its modularity, it was virtually impossible to use any kind of automated tests, because in order to run even a simple test you had to load the entire program. Hence, there was heavy reliance on manual testing.

Given the decision to disable dependency checking, which I definitely disagree with, this is a perfect example of a project where an early decision to rearchitect would have had a huge impact on long-term productivity and sustainability. On any project like this, the more time that passes, the harder the decision becomes to rearchitect, no matter how necessary it is.

The Good

The second example is of a project that started off with an aggressive deadline. The team shipped the product on time, but after shipping team members realized that their architecture had a number of problems. The largest was that the software was not easily testable, and as a result, there was too much reliance on manual testing. There was also a looming requirement for an Asian version of the product, and the version one software had not considered internationalization.

Luckily, the team did the right thing and made the necessary but difficult decision to rearchitect. The team first developed a design vision and a revised set of guiding principles for the design. They then spent their next two two-week iterations creating the new architecture and reworking their existing code into it. At the end of the second iteration, there were no new features, but two iterations after that, a record/playback feature was exposed that made a huge impact on testability. From that point, users were able to press record, do some work, and then press stop. Their work was saved in a file and could be read back in at any time for testing. This was a huge milestone for the project because it lessened the burden on people for testing and also made the developers more productive because now when they needed to recreate a problem they could simply load the user's file and start the playback.

Happily for this project, this team continues today to be highly productive and has managed to avoid any kind of defect backlog. This, despite the fact that their code has continued to grow in size *and* the development team is less than half the size it was for the first version.

Rearchitecture and Testability

Before you do the rearchitecture work, be sure you have added as many tests as possible as safeguards. You need to ensure that the new code behaves as expected. Unit tests should be a given and, if at all possible, add some integration tests to ensure that the new code provides the desired interfaces.

Without tests, the rearchitecture exercise could introduce so many problems that the benefits will be lost. Therefore, if you're going to do it, do it right and don't cut corners. If the code you are replacing has no tests, at least put a set of *good enough* tests in place so that your confidence is as high as possible that the new code behaves as expected.

There is no point in doing rearchitecture work if automated tests are not in place for all the new code. Think about ruthless testing and design testability into the new code!

PRACTICE 8: Design for Reuse

The topic of reusable software has somehow become the antithesis of agility, especially among many advocates of emergent design. And yet, the best way to enhance responsiveness to new opportunities is to have something to start from. If you have to start from scratch or are continually reinventing key algorithms, you are wasting effort, effort that should be spent concentrating on the new aspects of your project that will help you differentiate from what has already been done elsewhere.

Reusable software has fewer defects and cleaner interfaces than non-reusable software. Once a piece of software is used but not duplicated in more than one place, it is going to be tested twice, and likely in different ways. This makes the software more robust. When coupled with auto-mated tests of the interfaces for each use, the resulting software has a much greater chance of being extremely low in defects than if it were used only once.

The Business Value of Reusable Software

For many projects, reusable software directly speaks to business value. I was once involved in a project where we identified a market opportu-nity, but we had to deliver in less than six months. If we didn't deliver on time, the opportunity was gone. Luckily, we had two critical reusable software components. Their existence made it possible to deliver with minimal risk, and on time. As I told our executives later, if we had not had reusable software, we wouldn't have even been able to discuss the *possibility* of delivering the project.

Reusable software doesn't emerge. Although reuse can be arrived at through refactoring, there are often some key architectural decisions that need to be made as early as possible and carried through the project to make subsequent work much easier and less prone to needing to be redone. For example, when extensibility is important, it's wise to design the plug-in architecture early and then use it heavily, ideally so that all new features are developed as plug-ins. Without this up-front design and architecture work, the risk is that the system might be extensible, but not in a sustainable way.

Reuse is vital to sustainability because it minimizes wasted effort and allows new initiatives to be launched quickly. Unfortunately, it is only enabled by sound design and coding practices because you need to understand how to balance reuse against wasted effort.

I suspect the reaction to reuse stems from projects where software is overdesigned to make it reusable (which conflicts with simple design), resulting in a complex, defect-laden mess. This is where design intelligence comes in:

- If you aren't sure a piece of software is going to be reused, at least do everything you can to minimize coupling and dependencies with other software modules, ensure there are automated tests for the interfaces, and make it separately buildable (this is just common sense). This at least makes it easier for the next developer to get started and make the software truly reusable.
- If you know the software definitely won't be reused, don't use that as an excuse to ignore good design practices! (See the previous point.)
- *If you know that there is a high (>80%) likelihood of reuse, do it!* But keep the design and interfaces simple so that extension is possible when the code really is reused. Don't overdesign and waste effort on aspects of the implementation you don't immediately need and aren't certain of.

One of the largest problems and most important reasons to have reusable software is to eliminate duplicated code. It's tempting to just copy and paste a section of code, and although there may be a savings in effort in the short term, over the long term there will be a large amount of wasted effort. Duplicated code not only makes the size of the program larger, it also adds to complexity and is a common source of error, where a problem is fixed in one copy of the code but not another.

Reusable software also eases replaceability. If some portion of the architecture needs to be replaced, it is always easier to take out one section and change its interfaces as required than it is to try and replace the entire system. If there are no interface changes required, even better, because then at least you can reuse the automated tests on the interface to ensure your new implementation has the same behavior.

The notion of completely componentized software has been around since the introduction of Object-Oriented Programming. The notion of *software ICs* (i.e., software chips that can be wired together, much like chips on a printed circuit board) [Cox 1986] comes from the success of product line manufacturing. The automotive industry, for example, has reduced costs and defects by using as many common components (body panels, windshield wipers, motors, seats, instruments, etc.) as possible within a line of related vehicles.

Unfortunately, the ideal of fully componentized reuse as in manufacturing still largely eludes the software industry. I think this is because of the constant change in the software ecosystem and the level of overall complexity. However, despite the complexity, it is still possible to attain a high degree of reuse, and this aids sustainability by allowing teams to be more responsive to opportunities and to avoid duplicating effort. One of my hopes for open source software is that over time we can dramatically cut down on duplicated effort within the industry and allow a greater amount of common infrastructure to be developed and enhanced over time.

Summary

Design is vital to sustainable development because in order for software to last over the long term, it must be well designed. The problem, however, is that design is hard. There is a dilemma that every project faces and that is knowing when to design up-front and how much effort to invest in up-front design versus letting the design emerge. Good design practices should stress finding a balance between up-front and emergent design and emphasizing a collaborative design process that is not built around heavy requirements for documentation of the design.

I believe it is important to start with a vision and guiding principles for the design. These are the goalposts that team members must consider every day as they make tradeoffs. From there, the design practices should stress design iteration, constant change, design visibility, and collaboration. Mistakes are inevitably made, where software is over- or underdesigned. Software teams should rely on a focus on simplicity and a desire to avoid duplicated effort plus teamwork, knowledge, experience, and collaboration to reduce the number of mistakes and their severity. It is vital that design mistakes are fixed as quickly as possible, the appropriate lessons are learned, and then the team moves on. It is also critical that the team has the *guts* and *instincts* to make difficult decisions, such as to rearchitect before the cost of change becomes too high.

Continual Refinement

Chapter 7

Continual Refinement

In order to achieve sustainable development, teams need a way to balance short-term requirements and long-term needs: to ship their product as soon as they can while accepting, anticipating, and even welcoming change.

Software is complex and must evolve continuously over a long period of time. Throughout its life cycle, a software project must contend with changing user requirements in an evolving ecosystem of markets, partners, technology, and competition. In this environment, just about the only thing a software team can rely on is that change is a given. While some changes can be anticipated, teams must accept that most cannot; there are no crystal balls to predict the future. Experience with a particular software ecosystem can help, but it is still no guarantee for success. Therefore, teams must adopt a mindset and related practices that help them easily *adapt* to change as it happens while also *anticipating* change. The core agile software development practice of iterative development (described below) encourages continual refinement because it is a lightweight but formalized practice that helps teams adapt to and anticipate change.

In agile development, teams work from a simple and clear vision and deal with change through frequent iterations; the goal of each iteration is to deliver something useful to customers. Iterations begin with the team's laying a plan for upcoming iterations but with a focus on the next iteration. This planning takes into account the most recent available information such as an understanding of what the team has accomplished in past iterations (*velocity*, described below) customer feedback, or technology changes. The team then executes on the plan for the duration of the iteration, usually just a few weeks, delivers the software to the customer, and then takes a few moments to reflect and learn how it can further improve before planning and starting the next iteration. The agile methods keep the process as lightweight as possible so that the focus is placed on achieving results, while the tight feedback loop with customers encourages teams to do only what is most useful to the customers, which helps minimize wasted effort.

The main advantage of agile methods is that they help teams manage uncertainty and change early and throughout the project. However, while all agile projects combine aspects of anticipation and adaptation, poorly implemented agile methods can result in sloppy planning and reactive thinking [Highsmith 2004b]. Sloppy planning results when teams ignore information they already know or should know with minimal effort. Reactive thinking results when too much emphasis is placed on the team's ability to adapt to change. The result could be a project where lots of changes are being made but the amount of actual progress is low. Hence, the challenge with agile methods is to rely on *both* adaptability and anticipation and to have a team that knows when and how to apply each, and in what measure.

Traditional methods of software development rely too heavily on upfront planning and anticipation and virtually ignore adaptation. These approaches stress attempting to understand all user requirements and producing a detailed design before writing any software.

Agile methods are *not* the exact inverse of traditional methods; the common agile statement "we have more confidence in our ability to adapt than our ability to predict the future" should not be an excuse to ignore anticipation. Instead, in agile methods there must be an understanding of *good enough* anticipation. For example, spending a few days at the beginning of a project understanding user requirements or spending an hour every day discussing software design are worthy activities because they can cut down on rework and even, if done right, increase the ability of the team to adapt to change. The latter topic, especially as it applies to design, is dealt with in greater detail in Chapter 6 on Design Emphasis.

The need to involve both adaptation and anticipation in agile methods is similar to the need to consider both the short and long terms. In software projects, if too much emphasis is placed on the short-term, then software quality will suffer because the team will be continually reacting to crises and not being proactive. This will result in a continual degradation of the ability to adapt to change as described in Chapter 2. Equally as dangerous is when too much emphasis is placed on the long term (i.e., anticipation); these are the projects that are continually at risk of *never* shipping because they are unable to deal with changing user requirements through their emphasis on planning and design.

Agile Practices Are Still Useful When Adaptation Is Not Required

There are some projects where agility seems less important, where the temptation exists to stick with traditional approaches. Examples are where a software defect might lead to a loss of life or injury or the failure of an expensive piece of equipment such as in medical or aerospace applications, or in projects where milestones are tightly defined and must be approached in a given order. However, even in these projects there is value in lightweight collaborative planning and project tracking as described in this chapter, because virtually all projects can benefit from the steady rhythm and discipline of regular planning and tracking available in iterative development. Teams don't need to make changes to their plan in every iteration, but having the ability to change if needed could be the difference between a successful or failed project.

In my pre-agile days I was a believer in Microsoft Project and its Gantt charts. However, despite repeated attempts, I *never* produced a project schedule that stayed valid for more than a few weeks. If I didn't make an effort to create a new schedule every few weeks, then I would proceed blind and trust my instincts, and because creating a new schedule was so much work, I was probably flying blind more often than not. This is where a lightweight planning and tracking method as advocated by agile development would have been extremely useful.

PRACTICE 1: Iterative Development

Iterative development can be thought of as *plan a little, do a little, learn a little.* Iterative development is a core practice of sustainable software development because it gives the team a lightweight way to make *measurable* progress and to get feedback from customers as frequently and as *early* as possible. Getting feedback as early as possible is critical to ensuring that the system meets user requirements, that it is as simple as possible, and that there is minimal wasted effort. Minimizing wasted effort (features that users don't care about, features that are built in unusable ways, etc.) is an important business consideration because wasted effort has a cost and is inefficient.

Iterative development is amazingly simple. The schedule is broken up into a number of short equal-length iterations (2 to 6 weeks). At the end of each iteration, the software must be in a shippable state because it is given to customers for feedback. Each iteration has a little bit of planning, some real work is done, feedback is received from customers, the team records its progress to date, and reflects on how they can improve in the future.

Iterative development allows the team to replan and reprioritize at the beginning of every iteration. Planning is done in a lightweight but very effective manner using feature cards, with one feature card per feature. A feature card is a simple 3.5"x 5" index card. Because each iteration requires customer feedback, the team is able to keep its feature cards sorted into those that are done, those that are going to be worked on in the current iteration, and those that are going to be worked on in future iterations. Uncompleted features are arranged into a number of future iterations, and as the project proceeds, features will be added, removed, and reprioritized by the customer.

In iterative development, the feature cards and their arrangement into a number of iterations *is* the project schedule. The cards should be posted onto a board in a place that is accessible to the team. There are no detailed project schedules (PERT or Gantt charts), user requirement documents, etc. Instead, the feature cards contain all the documentation required to begin the work: a feature description[1], a time estimate, key acceptance criteria, risk (high, medium, low), and just about anything else that is useful to the team that will fit. One way to look at feature cards is that they are collaboration enablers: The cards themselves are less valuable than the conversations (and collaboration) that result from filling them out, moving them around, and understanding them. Hence, feature cards are meant to be *barely sufficient*, so that the team's emphasis is on producing a working product, not a stack of documentation.

Iterative development is important for sustainable development because it provides a regular *heartbeat* or checkpoint to the development effort. The regular rhythm is good for the team because it breaks the effort down into manageable pieces; it's good for project stakeholders and customers because they know they can expect to see progress on a regular basis [Cohn 2005]. Furthermore, since the goal of iterative development is to get feedback, teams are encouraged to keep the software in a working state; if the software is unreliable, then customers won't use it and can't give meaningful feedback. This topic of a Working Product is the focus of Chapter 4.

---

1. It takes a lot of practice to write good feature descriptions. See [Cohn 2004] for many good ideas.

Iterative Development Is a Good Technique for Open-Ended Research Projects

This is because research projects are almost always characterized by critical decisions as to whether to continue or halt exploration of a possible path to a solution. If a relatively short iteration time (2 to 4 weeks) is used, then the iteration reviews become an excellent forum to review the current progress and make continue/halt decisions.

This can be contrasted to managing a research project without this sense of time. In this case, it is often too easy to continue down "blind alleys" too long. Of course, iterations can often only be planned one at a time since there is minimal insight into future problems. However, since many false avenues are stopped earlier than they might otherwise be, research projects often produce results faster with iterative development than without!

Collaboration and Iterative Development

Iterative development is most effective when there is broad participation in iteration planning. At the beginning of each iteration, the entire team (business people, technical staff, and customers) has a short and intense iteration planning session. In this planning session the team analyzes and sorts the current set of desired features into an iteration plan based on risk (do the risky things early) and priority (determined by the customer). Tradeoffs are made through conversations within the team during the planning session.

Cross-functional collaboration is important to sustainable development because there is no hiding risk from any of the participants. Hence, active risk management is encouraged. Also, because it is a team exercise, everyone involved understands the current product status, what still needs to be accomplished, and also what can be accomplished in the time available. And because the planning is focused on providing value to customers real tradeoffs can be made, for example, between new features and making existing features work better for customers.

Iterative development is a humbling (in a good sense!) experience for the entire team. It's always easy to get enthused about a particular feature, but you can only introduce it once it is compared to the other features already in the plan. Collaboration helps to ensure that the right tradeoffs are made and the best possible priorities are set. There is no hiding the harsh reality that when someone wants to add a feature, in order to do so, another feature has to be removed from the plan!

Velocity

A key component of iterative development is the tracking of the project's *velocity*. Each feature card documents the time required to complete that feature in feature points. Feature points can be relative or absolute, though most people seem to prefer that feature points roughly equate to the number of ideal days of effort by a canonical developer. The card also documents the customer acceptance criteria; when these criteria have been met, the feature is completed. The velocity essentially is a record of the number of feature points completed in any given iteration.

Velocity is tracked throughout the project and gives an immediate indication of how well the project is (or is not) progressing. Incorporating velocity into the iteration planning sessions the team allows team members to make realistic plans for each iteration and also ask themselves difficult questions in cases where they are not making progress.

Given a record of velocity and the use of iterative development, all that team members really need to chart their progress is two charts that are easily maintained on a whiteboard or web page: velocity (by iteration) and number of feature points remaining. Some examples are shown in Figure 7-1. Although velocity cannot be compared between teams, within a team these two charts provide status of the project at a glance and a realistic gauge of when the project will complete based on the past and current progress[2].

Iteration 0

Iteration 0 is a short iteration (2 to 6 weeks) that the team can use to perform critical analysis work before starting actual development. Iteration 0 also

---

2. Although velocity cannot be compared between teams, the temptation to do so is very real. If people don't understand that every team and every project are different then it might be a good idea to estimate in relative points instead of days.

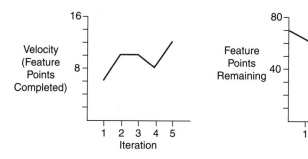

Figure 7-1
These two charts are sufficient for most projects to document and understand the state of their project. The chart on the left is a simple line chart that shows the velocity in each iteration. The chart on the right shows the number of feature points remaining in the project. By simply projecting a straight line and using the team's current and average velocity to date, the project team can visually determine when the product will ship with the current feature set. In this case, in iteration 7.

helps teams identify and document longer term considerations. Iteration 0 is an excellent time to:

- Ensure there is a project vision. A project vision is critical for any project, because the team must know what it is building. The vision helps the team make tradeoffs in its iteration planning meetings and also every day as members build the product.
- Create an initial release plan (see below). The release plan consists of what the team thinks is the minimum required set of features documented on feature cards and arranged into a number of iterations so that each iteration contains a target total number of feature points that does not exceed the current (or estimated) velocity.
- Create guiding principles for the design and the user experience. Guiding principles are described in more detail in Chapter 6.
- Create a design vision, high-level architecture, and key components of the architecture as described in Chapter 6.
- Write quick prototypes to understand critical features or risky areas better. Prototyping is described in Chapter 4.

PRACTICE 2: Release Planning

In order for iterative development to work, there must be a strong notion of a release. A release is a version of a product that can be installed and used by customers in their production environments. Usually, a release requires a number of iterations to build.

Release planning is important for sustainable development because it provides the longer term view that is necessary for planning purposes. Each project or release starts with *Iteration 0* (described previously), where the project vision and a plan that encompasses a number of iterations is laid out.

Once iteration 0 has been completed, the team should move into a build phase. The build phase consists of a number of iterations, with each iteration ending in a review with customers and planning for the next iteration.

During the build phase, the release plan that was created in iteration 0 must be periodically updated. Updates are required whenever the velocity changes or as the team identifies new features or determines that some features are not required. A common problem is that as new features are added to a project, other features are not dropped. This is why it is important to track the number of feature points remaining in the project, because when this happens it will be obvious that the project cannot complete on schedule given the current velocity as depicted in Figure 7-2. This is *good* because it forces the team to make tradeoffs frequently throughout the project as soon as a problem occurs rather than near the end of the release cycle (some call this *panic early, panic often*). The need to make tradeoffs also underlines why it is important to have business people involved in the planning, because as with any project, you can either change the date, the feature set, or the resources. You can't expect to fix all three. When businesspeople are involved in the planning, the types of tradeoffs that are possible during the release plan updates are obvious to them.

Figure 7-2
A case where the release plan must be reworked because all the features can't be completed on schedule. What has likely happened is that too many features have been added to the release plan and no features were dropped. The team must do one or more of the following: change the date, add some resources, or drop some features from the release plan.

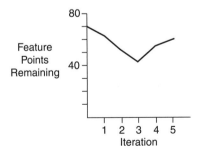

PRACTICE 3: Daily Standup Meetings

Hold a standup meeting the same time every day that is attended by the entire team—including businesspeople. The meeting should take an absolute maximum of 15 minutes (standing helps encourage this). The daily standup meeting is important for sustainable development because it helps to get issues out in the open each day, which helps to ensure that people aren't blocked for long periods of time and that everyone on the team is aware of what everyone else is doing. The traditional alternative is typically a weekly or monthly status meeting, and the problem with these meetings is that issues are often raised too late, that they're too long, and that the critical topics don't get raised.

In a daily standup meeting, each person answers three questions:

- What did you do yesterday?
- What are you going to do today?
- Are there any obstacles to your progress?

Keep track of time and limit discussion to ensure that the meeting finishes quickly. Invariably, issues come up during the meeting that can be dealt with immediately after the scrum by those who are interested.

Standup meetings are highly effective at gathering status, getting important issues out into the open, and encouraging collaboration among the team. The most effective way to solve problems when more than one person needs to be involved is face-to-face rather than in e-mail; the standup meeting, and the collaboration that happens immediately after, is an aid to the critical issues being dealt with face-to-face immediately.

It is also important that daily standups lead to solving the problems of the moment immediately after the standup is finished. Weekly status report meetings are not nearly as effective because many problems are no longer immediate and the delay is a potential killer of team momentum. Likewise, e-mail can have a similar effect because there is a disconnect between the raising of the problem and any possible solution. Of course, there are always impromptu meetings, and some problems will still require these, but the existence of the daily standup means that team members know there is a forum where they can get these issues out in the open easily.

Daily Standup Meetings and Discipline

As with any type of meeting, daily standups require discipline. Time discipline and topic discipline are the hardest things to master with daily standup meetings.

One team I worked with had daily standups that lasted more than an hour! It's too easy to want to dive into a topic during the standup; someone has to suggest that people who are interested can get together after the standup meeting. It makes sense to have someone in charge of the meeting to get it started and to truncate discussions that are clearly going to take too long.

It's also hard to know how much to say when it's your turn in the standup meeting. I've seen people that default to saying too little, so that some of the obstacles aren't brought up, and also people who say too much so that too much detail is outlined. Again, this is where it makes sense to have someone in charge of the meeting, to both prompt with questions for more detail and also to provide feedback to people after the standup if they provide too much detail.

PRACTICE 4: Retrospectives

Retrospectives [Kerth 2001] are a critical part of sustainable software development. In order for continual refinement to be effective, the team must be able to continually learn and adjust not only its project (*what* the team is building) but also the methods members use (*how* the team works).

Teams should hold retrospective meetings at regular intervals during their projects. Ideally, this would be at the end of every iteration or the end of every second or third iteration. The purposes of these retrospectives are to provide a forum where the teams can openly question their current development processes and progress, learn from their mistakes and failures, and decide what changes they need to make to proceed effectively.

One of the key aspects of a retrospective is that you *must* lay out ground rules in advance. It is vital that a retrospective be a positive experience that focuses on learning and not on laying blame. Start by assuming that everyone on the team is doing the best he or she can, with the recognition that there is always room for improvement for every member of the team. Ideally, retrospectives should help uncover areas for improvement and give every-one ideas as to how to contribute more strongly to the project. But retro-spectives should never be personal or antagonistic—keep those discussions private and behind closed doors.

Retrospectives are a simple mechanism that helps increase the chance of your project's success. Frequent retrospectives during your project help ensure that course corrections and changes to your project and processes are made when you need to make them, not after it is too late. When action is required, the next retrospective should uncover what was not completed and why.

Retrospectives also serve as a useful forum to help the team bond because it gives them ownership of their processes with an eye to continual improvement. Team members aren't being told how to do their work—they are committing to each other how they are going to work. There is a huge difference between being told and making a commitment to your peers!

A simple format for the retrospective is to first ensure that the *entire* team is present (including businesspeople), select a moderator (ideally neutral, such as from another team), and then answer some basic questions such as:

- What worked well?
- What needs to be improved?
- What should we do differently?

Then, review outstanding action items from previous retrospectives and develop a new set of action items and changes that will be put in place immediately. Be sure to document your results and archive them in a central location so you can refer to them later.

TIP   Be Creative!

There are many creative things you can do to make retrospec-tives more productive and fun. For example, use different col-ored sticky notes to capture issues of differing levels of priority. Use a teddy bear or similar object to control who is speaking. Or capture an image of the screen of the product at each retrospec-tive. It can be a lot of fun in the retrospective at the end of the project to review these images and notice how much the product has changed and evolved.

The duration of retrospectives is a variable that must be carefully monitored to ensure they do not become a burdensome overhead. Frequent checkpoint retrospectives that are held during a project should take an hour or less, while retrospectives held at the end of a major release might take a day or more, depending on how elaborate a retrospective is required.

Traditional Methods: Plan a Lot, Do a Lot, Learn a Little

Traditional methods of software development are best termed *plan a lot, do a lot, learn a little*. Great effort is spent before any software is written to understand the user's requirements and design the system. Then it is built, usually with little or no customer feedback.

Customer feedback usually doesn't occur until a beta version is released to select customers. But beta releases are almost always too late to do anything about customer-reported issues or requests because they're usually late in the release cycle. Because customer feedback is late in the release cycle, there is a high chance of wasted effort as features that aren't critical to customers are built or features are built in ways that aren't usable. And because customer requests often lead to risky changes that would jeopardize the eventual release, they often get moved into the next release, when in most cases the changes will be less useful, not to mention late!

Usually, teams are so busy building their products and trying to meet their deadlines that they hold a post-mortem at the completion of the project. But along the way, they have missed many opportunities for course correction and process changes.

PRACTICE 5: Coaching and Team Development

Coaching and team development are important for continual refinement to help the team achieve the best possible results while collaborating together and with customers. Coaching is an interpersonal skill that helps people provide each other with real-time feedback so they can do their work more effectively. Real-time feedback is important for continual refinement because it ensures problems are dealt with as quickly as possible. Team development (understanding the business and professional development) are equally important because the more the team understands the business and has current skills, the better it will be at both anticipating and initiating changes in its ecosystem.

Coaching

Coaching is an important interpersonal skill for every member of the team. Coaching is essentially providing individuals (people who work for you, people you report to, and people you work with), teams, and customers the real-time feedback they need to become more effective and continually improve. Coaching helps minimize friction and negative tensions while helping people work better together and focus on the desired result.

Understanding the Business

Understanding your company's business is an important element of sustainable development. The knowledge gained through this understanding is vital in anticipating and understanding changes to the ecosystem your project is dependent on. While some would argue that software developers should focus on writing code, I believe that this too often results in undesirable side effects, such as:

- *Team members who don't understand what is valuable to their customers and why, even when told.* This is often because they do not understand how the customers use the product and hence what is important to them.
- *People who cannot listen to customers and understand what they are really asking for.* Understanding what the customer is trying to do is critical because users most often ask for alterations to their current workflow only, when perhaps the problem is the workflow itself.
- *People who don't understand what provides value to customers.* Sometimes, work that provides value to customers is mundane, but it must be done.

- *People who don't understand the economics of their business.* How does your company make its money? Sometimes, customers ask for major features. If you always listen to your customers, then they will get everything for free. Your company needs to stay in business, though, and it may be more desirable to sell the customer a new product or add on to an existing product.
- *In companies with multiple products, especially where there is overlapping functionality, it is common for people on each team to want to add all features their customers ask for to their product when in fact only one of the products may need it.* Also, where multiple products serve the needs of a single customer or market segment, there may be detrimental competition between the product teams; these teams need a major wake-up call to realize that the competition they need to be concerned with is outside their company!
- *People who don't understand the economics of their markets.* Too many technically brilliant products are conceived to address what may be a sexy or obvious opportunity, which unfortunately is not viable economically due to a small target market or unrealistic pricing. Other problems may be misunderstanding the technical sophistication of users and building a solution that is too complex or too simple for them. Or, developers may not understand the economic reality of their customers where, for example, end-users may not value a software product at a realistic level because they (the end-user) are faced with massive costs in other areas that dwarf any potential for software.
- *Teams that don't pay attention to their development processes.* I have seen too many projects, where due to a whole range of factors such as poor planning and design, sloppy programming practices, a lack of risk analysis, defect backlogs, etc., a project team is required that is too large for the size of the target market. These are projects that are quickly cancelled, because the investment does not justify the returns: i.e., why should a company invest in a project with lower returns than if it was to take the money and put it in a bank account to collect interest?
- If the only value you provide to an organization is writing code, then your job can be outsourced (i.e., worked on by cheaper labor).

You need to understand your company's markets, users, competition, and financials. You won't always have access to all this information down to the finest level of detail, but you should have enough access to ask intelligent questions or be able to ask questions to get some information. Don't look upon it as "management's" responsibility to give you this information; effective communication goes both ways. People in management are almost always too immersed in the details of the business to realize what type of information you need.

My largest observation of people who work in most companies today is that they are too isolated from customers. Try to visit your customers or at least ask people who do visit customers to write up reports or give a short talk about what they learned. Bring your customers to visit you as often as you can.

Direct Customer Contact Helps Create a Balanced View

Recently, one of my co-workers went to a trade show and attended a user forum for the product he works on. He went in thinking he had better bring a bulletproof jacket because all he had seen were defect reports and postings on user forums. He came back completely rejuvenated and very positive. Sure, there were some unhappy customers but even they said, "Hey, I know I complain about your product, but it rocks. I couldn't do without it!".

Project teams often get a distorted view of their work if they don't have enough direct customer contact. This is because it is human nature to want to report problems and to say nothing when things are going well, and customers are human. Since most problem reports are done through impersonal e-mail or web forms, it is also human nature for many people to be less diplomatic than they should be—problems are frustrating after all. If all a product team sees are the defects that customers report and negative e-mails, then the team is likely lacking a balanced view of what customers *really* think.

One of the things I have little tolerance for is a software team that insists it needs to completely rewrite the product. Too many developers don't understand the company's need to stay in business. The problem, of course, is that it's always easier to write code than to read it, especially when you didn't write it. And it's no fun just fixing bugs in someone else's code. But few companies in the software industry can afford to start again from scratch. That's why teams should be encouraged to rewrite parts of their products as required and aggressively and constantly refactor as recommended in Chapter 6. The alternative is not pretty: While a product is being rewritten, your competition is developing new features while you are effectively standing still. Even if you build in new features, you are still going to be behind simply because of the lost market share. People who *get* this are highly treasured by organizations (or at least should be!).

Professional Development

Professional development is important for both personal and project reasons [Hunt and Thomas 2000] [Hohmann 1996]. From a project standpoint, teams that are knowledgeable in as many areas as possible, even those that are seemingly unrelated to the current project, have the best chance of succeeding at sustainable development. The reason for this is simple: These teams have a varied set of skills and knowledge, a rich tool chest if you will, that can be drawn from and applied with maximal effect. Professional development is vital to ensure that the team has all the skills it needs to understand its ecosystem of markets, competition, and underlying technologies.

At a personal level, your skills are vital to your team's success and to yours. It is your responsibility to ensure you are continually improving in your profession. You can't rely on anyone else to tell you to take courses or read or learn. You have to be proactive. You can't blame anyone else if your career does not progress as you would like. Read, take training courses, experiment with new programming languages and approaches to problems, and above all learn, collaborate, mentor, and teach.

PRACTICE 6: Make Key Metrics Visible

Every project should collect some key metrics and find ways to make them visible to the project team. Visibility might be achieved by a simple web page or maybe even a big visible chart on a whiteboard or by the water cooler. The reason metrics are helpful is that they can, if they are presented in the right way, help the team focus on keeping important aspects of its project under control. Metrics help the team track its progress on a regular basis and get early warning signs when problems are beginning to develop. Entire books have been written on the subject of metrics, and I think sometimes people get carried away. A small set of simple metrics should suffice, and if their collection and display can be automated, then your team will be in good shape to continually monitor and improve its progress.

An overlooked aspect of metrics is that they enhance learning. By making them visible, they help drive meaningful discussions about the trends and how to change or improve the trends. If done in a positive way, these conversations help drive the collaborative problem solving that is invaluable to the team. Of course, if metrics are implemented in a negative way, such as by tracking individual instead of team metrics, then you can expect the opposite effect.

Some example metrics might be:

- *Charts of velocity and feature points remaining* (as described above).
- *A chart that shows the status of all system tests, and how long they took to run.* This helps to catch system and performance problems early and prevents cases where the system tests don't run.
- *A graph that shows the amount of time required for nightly build(s).* This helps to keep the builds as small and fast as possible, which is a critical issue to ensure developers are as productive as possible: Slow builds mean lower productivity.
- *A graph that shows the number of outstanding (not fixed) defects, by severity.* Outstanding defects are a key indicator of sustainable development. Teams cannot carry around large backlogs of defects and should fix as they go.
- *A graph that shows the number of incoming defects, by severity over time.* This is an indicator of how well tested the product was. High incoming rates might lead teams to set aside more time for fixing defects in the short term, or perhaps help point to areas of the product that need refactoring/replacement.
- *A graph that shows the number of fixed defects per week over time.*
- *A companion to the previous two graphs (incoming and fixed defects) is a graph that shows the net gain.* The net gain is essentially incoming minus fixed, which should always be around 0 and as close as possible to a flat line.

- *A chart that tracks the amount of source code versus test code.* This gives team members visible evidence that they are adding enough tests as their source code grows.
- A chart that shows defect density, in terms of number of defects (on average) per thousand lines of code.

Summary

Continual refinement is an important principle for sustainable development because it enables teams to both adapt to and anticipate change in *what* they are doing (their project) and *how* they are doing it. Teams break down their projects into short, manageable iterations. The advantage of breaking down work in this way is that complexity is much easier to manage in small slices, and immediate feedback from users provides the teams with a powerful way to change directions if they need to. In addition, teams employ regular retrospectives so that they can talk about their projects in an open and honest way. This allows them to make adjustments to their processes, which is equally important to sustainability because continual learning and improvement help ensure the project will last over the long term.

Chapter 8

Culture Change
and Sustainable
Development

It is highly likely that in order for your organization or team to achieve sustainable development, a new product development culture is required. I feel this chapter is necessary because I have seen too many situations where enthusiastic people with great ideas are stymied, consciously or unconsciously, by their organizations.

Too few people consider how to introduce change to their colleagues and management and how to make the changes last. So-called change agents almost always have a great deal of enthusiasm, but they often take on the entire burden of change themselves, hit a stumbling block or opposition, and then do one of many things: retreat into a shell, lash out, get burned out, or find another job. Many organizations, usually unknowingly, have a built-in immune system that can quickly stifle change. But even in these situations change is not impossible if you understand the dynamics of the people in the organization.

Where change is required, there is the significant challenge of achieving *lasting change*. It's easy for people to try out something new, but as soon as something goes wrong, the most common reaction is to revert to what was known to work in the past—even if it doesn't really work. Lasting change requires changes to what is measured, recognized, rewarded, and reinforced. For example, many companies recognize people who work long hours and who are independent project heroes, whereas in a sustainable development culture, it would be more valuable to recognize people who find innovative ways to achieve technical collaboration on their projects and make the people around them more effective.

Achieving lasting culture change is hard. It takes a lot of determination, vision, *and* persistence. Principles and practices aren't good enough because people define culture. And people are complex and unique. Therefore, it is unrealistic to expect that a sustainable software development culture can be so clearly defined that it is identical in every instance. In fact, the opposite is true; we should expect sustainable development cultures to be *different* simply because of the people involved, and these differences will manifest themselves through variations in how practices are applied.

There are two change scenarios of interest in this chapter: sustainable development on a new project and turning a project that is on the unsustainable path into sustainable. These situations are obviously unique and require variations in approach. This chapter is therefore broken up into three parts: the common topic of making change happen, followed by a discussion of the unique aspects of the two scenarios.

Understanding

The primary challenge in attempting culture change is in understanding the dynamics of each unique situation and the people, culture, and environment, then using this knowledge to determine how change can be first started and then maintained in a highly collaborative way.

Cynics can easily read a chapter like this and come away with the impression that leadership and introducing change involves manipulation. But you need to apply a filter as you read. Think about the importance of *truly* understanding the situation and about how critical *positive* collaboration and engaging others is. You often have to help people understand their current situation and what the possibilities are, and you have to help *influence* the change, but you can't do it alone. Forget about manipulation and command-control; they won't work!

Making Change Happen

Many good books are available on how to make change happen in an organization. For reference, I've included some of my favorites in Appendix 4.

I wish it were possible to provide a template for making change happen. Something along the lines of: If you're a programmer and want to change your organization to sustainable development, do this, then that, say this, etc. My personal experience with leading change has been that every organization is different, that this is particularly true of software organizations, and that software organizations are especially difficult to change. The problem I think stems from many factors, including:

- *Software people come from many backgrounds.* I've worked with people who have degrees in engineering, physics, mathematics, astrophysics, computer science, psychology, sociology, English, music, business, and accounting. Many of my co-workers have had multiple degrees; some have even had no degrees.
- In many organizations people who understand amazingly little about software development, sometimes appallingly so, wind up managing the organization. **Note:** I'm not necessarily saying this is a problem. I have worked for some managers who are excellent at knowing what they don't know and who to ask—although I've also worked for managers who don't, which is a problem. It's difficult to find good managers who love both business and software development. Usually, people with a sales or financial background and/or people who have written a few lines of code sometime in the past are the ones who wind up in control because they tend to be more extroverted and/or charismatic than most technical people. Management is only a problem when it is bad or incompetent.
- Many organizations do not discuss or try to consciously foster their culture and development practices or pay attention to key people issues such as professional development and leadership. Instead, they focus on projects, schedules, and results. While there is no question that results are important, if the bottom line is the main focus then there is a problem.
- There are a lot of incredibly bright people in software organizations. On just about any topic of importance there will be no shortage of opinions. This can be both good and bad depending on the topic at hand, and it can lead to situations where creating consensus is difficult or even impossible. However, being bright in a problem-solving sense doesn't necessarily translate into being a good communicator. Many people in software organizations are good talkers

but not listeners, and some are not very good at expressing their opinions in a respectful way. Hence, while having a group of bright people may seem like a good thing, when it comes to making change happen, sometimes the fact that everyone has an opinion and that some people are poor at expressing their opinions means that resistance to change can be quite high. Or, resistance might just seem high because people are usually very good at expressing displeasure but not as proactive as they should be at providing positive feedback.

- Software education lacks standards and a poor understanding of what the basics are. Most people learn more about software development on the job than they do in school because only in the workplace are they confronted with the task of maintaining a million lines of code for ten years or joining projects where a large amount of code already exists and the people who wrote it are no longer available. I also know people who have graduated from top universities in computer science who have been well schooled in theory such as NP complete problems but haven't taken a course in compilers or computer construction!

- People don't like being told how to work. They want to be able to choose the best approach based on learning. Hence, the challenge with achieving culture change is finding ways to achieve complete buy-in and then helping and providing advice as required.

- People are different. Consider this basic list of character traits: introvert, extravert, opinionated, stubborn, consensus-builder, excitable, emotional, and restrained. Software developers tend to be introverts. Sales and marketing people tend to be extraverts. Add age as a factor as well: Older and more experienced workers tend to be more jaded by past experiences (or perhaps they are just more relaxed).

- Organizations are complex simply because of the mix of different people, for better and worse. What will work in one organization likely will not work in another.

- Complacency. We almost always underestimate the effort required to introduce change into an organization. Complacency is often at the heart of failed change efforts because if your co-workers don't understand the need for change they won't actively participate.

- It's hard to admit that you have to change, too. We tend to generalize when things get uncomfortable. Driving a car is a perfect example.

When asked, we consistently say that there are too many jerks on the road and that other drivers cause the problems. And yet that clearly can't be the case because someone has to be the other driver. Few people admit that they need to improve their driving skills when actually we should all be continually striving to get better.

- Try this experiment with your co-workers. Have all of them cover their eyes and ask people to raise their hands if they believe they are open to change. Then, with eyes still covered, ask people to raise their hands if they believe other people are unwilling to change. What you will invariably see is that virtually every hand will be raised in response to both questions! The implication should be obvious: that while you may think you are open to change, the impression you give to other people may be different. Change has to *start* with you and it is *your* responsibility to find ways to engage others.

None of these factors is catastrophic. They're really just the people factors you need to keep in mind when considering how to introduce change into your organization. People, and the culture they have built for themselves, are probably the largest variable between organizations. People and culture are also the largest potential barriers to change. You have to recognize that any change challenges the comforts that have been built up over time.

Change Factors and Enablers

In order to create change, I believe the following *change factors* must be present:

- Leadership
- A sense of urgency
- Executive support

And the following *change enablers* enable the overall change effort:

- Persistence
- Training
- Continual "wins"

Figure 8-1
The reaction people have to any change initiative is most likely going to take the form of a bell curve (or normal) distribution. Some people are going to be apathetic or be openly resistant, and others are going to be enthusiastic and want to get to it. Most reactions are going to fall somewhere in between, and the factors that are going to influence whether the bulk of the people are going to resist or enthusiastically support the changes are whether there is a sense of urgency that everyone can identify with, the degree of executive support, and the involvement of key leaders at every level in the organization.

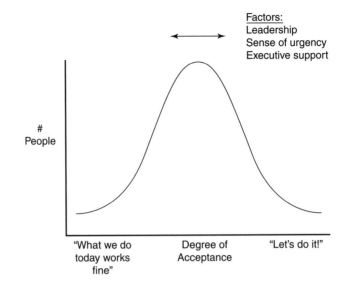

- Positive reinforcement of desired behaviors
- Communication, vision, and strategy

Each of the above topics is covered in detail below.

In my experience, you're going to get acceptance or resistance in varying degrees that usually resembles a bell curve, as illustrated in Figure 8-1. The point is that it's very rare that you can convince everyone right away, but you can influence how the changes will be perceived and accepted by the majority of people. And most importantly, you can't manipulate people, but you can engage them.

Change Factors

Leadership

Leadership, for some reason, is a term that many people shy away from. Perhaps this is because of the negative connotation: that leaders are the senior managers in the company and that leadership is hence top-down. Certainly, many management books are written that way, with the need for change coming from the CEO or senior management, and various techniques such as strategic goal setting and coaching are employed to get the organization on board and steer the right course. The other extreme is the bottom-up approach, where change is initiated at the very lowest level of the organization and then percolates up through the hierarchy. This is often how Extreme Programming gets started in an organization, with a software team trying it out and then the practices being adopted by other teams. The common thread in both these extremes is that no single person can make change happen.

In order for any change to succeed, there must be *leadership at all levels*. Change starts with individual leaders. These are people who realize that change has to start with what they can control: themselves. They start change by first occupying a new space themselves, then finding ways to get other people (their co-workers, their boss, their team, and their subordinates) to *want* to occupy that space with them, and then helping them to do so. By this definition, there are leaders at many levels in an organization, from the programmer who prods her co-workers and team leader into using automated tests, the team leader or coach who helps his team achieve its best work and ship a product, the product manager who works with users to ensure they understand the importance of their input, to the CEO who leverages the expertise of her teams to set the business goals for the organization. The trick in making change happen is finding as many leaders as possible and at as many levels of the organizations as possible, developing and empowering them, and getting them actively involved in the change process.

Sense of Urgency

Change won't happen unless people understand and agree with the need for change. One of the most important tasks before trying to initiate change is to develop a message that clearly and emphatically states the need for change. The new way can't just be better; it has to make a positive difference to everyone in the organization and its customers, and by extension to the company's bottom line.

Know Your Audience

One of the key aspects of developing a sense of urgency is having a message that can be tuned to the audience. Executives and senior

---

managers need to have a completely different understanding of the need for change than developers or QA people, for example. Your ability to communicate to the various audiences will help determine how much importance will be placed on the change initiative.

Executive Support

Change can happen without executive support, but the more executive support there is, the easier the change effort will be. An executive is really anyone who controls the ability to spend money and helps steer company policy—the higher in the organization, the better. Executives can help free up funds and people's time for training; they can also help with communication and rewarding desired behaviors. A word of warning: It may also be necessary to convince executives that they need to change, too—for example, if their style is overbearing or if they are unable to collaborate.

Change Enablers

Persistence

With any change, there are going to be peaks and valleys in effort, performance, and results. You have to go in *knowing* that these are going to occur and that you will need continual effort over a long period of time. The peaks are going to be periods of time where it will be easy to relax and relish success too much, when what you really need is a new set of goals that push you on to even greater accomplishments. The valleys are by far the most trying periods, where it seems like everyone is ignoring the message or reverting to their old ways. It is completely natural for people to revert to the familiar during trying periods because the familiar ways are going to be more comfortable than new approaches. A common valley in a change initiative is at the beginning (remember the chemical manufacturing example in Chapter 1), where there is a dip in performance as the team deals with all the same problems using new approaches. These are the times where leaders must lead, to ensure that the organization doesn't get too comfortable when everything is going well and overreact when it's not.

Team Sports and Persistence

Competitive team sports are an example of the need for persistence. Great leaders in sport (coaches *and* players) are those who help their teams keep their composure during games so that they are always mentally *in the game*.

If the team is winning, it must not let up or its opponent will come back. If the team is losing, it needs to never give up and not get so desperate to make a play that players commit mental mistakes. Likewise, if a player commits an error, he or she can't afford to sulk or lay blame; instead that player needs to admit the mistake, learn from it, and be ready for the next opportunity. And celebration of success is important, but not if it leads to a false sense of security.

The most physically gifted team does not always win. Too many teams build a lead then relax. Or they celebrate a victory prematurely. Or they let one or two losses in a row erode their confidence. Or they commit stupid penalties at crucial times. Great teams win because they're persistent, and they don't let the peaks or the valleys affect them through being disciplined.

Training

Training is often vital to help people learn new skills and understand new methods. It can be done by bringing consultants in (external training) or using your own people (internal training). Each type of training has its own advantages and disadvantages, but the key factor is that whoever leads the training has to have credibility with the audience. External consultants should be carefully selected to ensure that your organization is maximizing its investment by having the best experts with the deepest expertise (and credibility) possible.

Internal training may seem like a luxury because it requires that people have time to prepare the course material. However, in my experience, it can be powerful and effective, especially when one of the organization's respected leaders puts together appropriate material where he or she can pass on important experiences or dive into a topic that is relevant to the organization.

Training topics should be carefully chosen. To introduce sustainable development into an organization, I recommend a minimum of training on agile project management, hands-on technical training for technical staff, plus some kind of executive training to give an overview of the methods being introduced and the business rationale behind them.

The Value of External Consultants

External consultants are often invaluable to assist with training and establishing a sense of urgency. They bring experiences from other companies, and these experiences help them communicate successful strategies employed.

Also, sometimes what an external consultant says will hold more weight than an internal employee. Often, having an external and *neutral* voice ask a hard question that has been asked a million times before by employees is enough to shake people out of their sense of complacency. Hence, especially for larger organizations, I highly recommend that you identify and hire an experienced consultant who will have credibility in your organization.

Continual "Wins"

The most important thing to aim for is to produce continual "wins." These can be in the form of new tests, new tools, changes in defect trends, successful projects, or whatever is meaningful to your company. They are particularly vital in the early days of change and should be targeted as soon as possible, mostly to ensure that people see that change is possible and that it is recognized (via communication). You cannot expect change to happen quickly, and so you must use the continual wins to reinforce success and keep everyone aware of the fact that progress is being made.

Positive Reinforcement of Desired Behaviors

Change requires new behaviors that must replace existing behaviors. For example, here are some of the common behavior changes required when introducing sustainable development to an organization:

- Project leaders must be able to create an environment where everyone participates in iteration planning. In many organizations the role of the project leader is to identify the tasks that must be completed, collect estimates from the developers, create a schedule, and then track progress against the schedule.

- Refactoring and rewriting must be fully supported by everyone in the organization.
- People must learn to resist the pressure to get features done. If the product is not in a working state, what's the point in completing the feature and adding to the problem?
- In many organizations, executives or product managers have the most contact with customers and teams are insulated from the "demands" of customers. It's almost always best to set up direct and frequent collaboration with customers.
- Developers must write tests and work at defect prevention. If developers are still rewarded for the number of hours they work and features they churn out, regardless of quality, they will not embrace their role in defect prevention, and no culture change will result because they will still look to a testing or QA organization or customers to find problems.
- People must collaborate. If heroes are rewarded for saving projects and acting as prima donnas, then collaboration will be less important than being a hero.

Communication

Lots of positive and well-timed communication is a critical change enabler. At every company I have worked at, communication has been identified by employees as one of the principal shortcomings of the organization or management team. I think this is a reflection of the fact that you can never communicate enough.

The purpose of communication during change is to keep people excited and in tune with the importance of the changes. It is possible to communicate too much, which is why it is very important to think about the timing of your communication. Definitely talk about the continual wins the team has achieved and recognize that over time things will begin to look drier and less exciting. Those are the points where you may need to set a new set of goals or get some new people involved or find some new ways to get the message out.

Start with What You Can Control and Influence

A metaphor for how to get started in turning around a project is catching up on e-mail after an extended absence such as a vacation. The way I deal with this situation is I start with what I can control, which is the e-mail I receive the day I return. This ensures that the backlog doesn't get any worse while I work on older messages. I will first look for recent high-priority messages and deal with those. Then, as time permits, I will start by deleting (without reading) messages that are clearly junk or out of date. I will then look for mail threads (i.e., multiple messages with the same subject) and start by reading the most recent message on the thread. In most cases, I can then delete all the older messages and be caught up on the subject. By the time I've finished this process, very few messages will be left, and life will be back to normal because I'll be caught up.

Moving to a culture of sustainability is obviously not the same nor is it as simple as dealing with an e-mail backlog. However, if you are able to recognize that you need to start with what you can control, know where you want to end up, and have an understanding of the steps you can take to get yourself out of the current situation, then the change scenario becomes more plausible. You can't try to solve everything at once, and you need to think about the problem in understandable increments that keep you on the desired path. Change initiatives will fail if they attempt to *boil the ocean* or lack focus or a clear sense of first steps and overall vision.

Think of your organization as a supertanker; it is big and takes a long time to change direction. Given that you know where you want to end up, recognize that you can't make the entire turn at once. Instead, what are the things you can do at any point in time that nudge the supertanker in the desired direction?

Avoid Transition Plans

In my opinion, one of the most common mistakes made when introducing change is to use a transition plan. In my experience, they don't work. The problem with transition plans is it is common to rationalize reasons for why the transition plan cannot be followed, such as a recession or a critical project or feature that must be completed first. Typically, transition plans are something that can be put in place *later* or are somehow optional. Later may never come. There must be a strong desire for change, and change often means taking a risk or being aggressive. Transition plans are rarely risky or aggressive.

An analogy that one of my colleagues came up with is losing weight. In order to lose weight, you can't *talk* about the need to lose weight and the need to change your lifestyle by eating better and exercising regularly. Successful weight loss is *doing it,* not talking about it, *starting immediately* not at some time in the future or by phasing in better food and more exercise.

Turning Unsustainable into Sustainable Development

If you are working on a project that is on the unsustainable development curve, the most important thing you must recognize is that you can't just "blow up" your current processes and practices. That would most likely lead to disaster. Next, you need to recognize that achieving sustainable development is going to take time, and probably more time than you think. You also have to recognize that you are going to have to make compromises and can't strive for perfection; you likely won't ever have the architecture you'd like or have tests in place for every single line of code. Just think about getting continually better over time, in tiny increments if need be.

If you can, start with a small team. Then, use the successes and knowledge gained in that team to get other teams involved. You might want to consider moving people between teams if you can. New people added to a highly efficient team will be able to learn the new principles quickly. However, you need to be careful when moving people from the "model" team to other teams because they can easily get buried in the day-to-day reality of their new team unless they are strong, persistent leaders/coaches or can be moved in pairs or sub-teams. You might want to think of these sub-teams as a "tiger team", that can be added to any project and lead change by example. But these people must *not* think of themselves as better or superior.

Unsustainable projects, or those on the path to unsustainability, are likely going to have a few key problems that are going to need targeting. Most likely, these will include aspects such as:

- Legacy code that is poorly structured and has many broken windows.
- Inadequate or nonexistent test coverage.
- Attitudes that result in the use of phrases like "ship to QA" or "throw it over the wall for testing." These are indicators of a defect detection culture, where developers are not doing enough testing themselves.
- Entrenched development practices and attitudes that are counter to what is required. The longer practices have been used, the harder it is to change them and the easier it is for people to go back to them at the first sign of trouble or stress.
- Defect rates that are unsustainable and increasing.
- Bureaucratic project management practices that emphasize planning and tracking progress against the plan.
- A lack of understanding of the current development problems and visibility into their magnitude.

Where to Begin

Assuming that you have buy-in to change and have decided on your approach (training, consultants, etc.), where do you begin? Start by analyzing the mindset of your organization and mapping it against the four principles: continual refinement, working product, defect prevention, and design emphasis. Given that your early goal is going to be building wins, the following practices can be used to produce results quickly:

- You can get an errant project back on track quickly using the **agile project management practices** simply by beginning iterative development, tracking your velocity, using daily standup meetings, and **retrospectives**.
- Start **ruthless testing** by emphasizing unit tests for new code and, if you can, by putting safeguards in place such as system level tests to catch regressions sooner.

- Introduce **simple design** and **refactoring**.
- If you aren't already doing so, make sure your product is **built nightly** (completely, from scratch) and that you are using a **configuration management system**.
- Pay attention to your **design practices**. If you do a lot of up-front design currently, don't stop doing design because you don't think it's agile. Don't get hung up on simple design and emergent design. Start with **frequent rapid design meetings** and architectural reviews.
- Make sure you have a defect tracking system in place and that you are rigorously tracking defects. Then, start collecting some **metrics** to find out what kind of defect trend and backlog you have. This will help plan your next steps to help get defects under control.
- As you become familiar with the new practices, use your retrospectives as a way to review the practices from this book (or any other good source) and introduce new practices as you see fit.

The Three Phases of Change

There are three phases that a change initiative goes through. Each phase has its unique challenges and pitfalls. It helps to be aware of which phase you think your change initiative is in so the team can have realistic expectations and goals.

1. In the initial phase, the challenge is to get started and to develop the first wins. A common failure in this stage is to have expectations that are too high and then to give up when they aren't met. Enthusiasm has to be high in at least a core group of people to make a difference. It may be a good idea to form a guiding council to channel the initial enthusiasm.

2. In the second phase, the challenge is to work through the inevitable peaks and valleys of enthusiasm and results. A common failure in this stage is to assume the job is done, wrap everything up, and then a few months later realize that too many old behaviors are coming back.

3. The third phase is one of ongoing maintenance. The main goal in this phase is to simply ensure that the keystone principles and practices are in place and that there is continual learning and improvement. Probably the most common failure in this

stage is to lose discipline on a keystone practice such as retrospectives so that opportunities to learn and improve are missed.

Sustainable Development for New Projects

In many ways, introducing sustainable development principles and practices for a new project is going to be easier than on an established project. Teams on new projects are almost always determined to do things the right way. It's going to be possible, for example, to employ ruthless testing by having good test coverage and building testability into your project.

However, new projects are often launched with unrealistic expectations, or they are too ambitious. If you're going to start with new practices, I recommend you start with the keystone practices from Appendix 1 and then use your retrospectives to tune and add to your processes over time.

Another problem with new projects is that people are often trying out new practices for the first time. I have found that it's vital to have the team talk about its practices in an open way, especially through the initial phases. For example, I worked with one team where the team embraced simple design, but a few developers had read a XP book and thought simple design meant *no* up-front design. This resulted in some of the code being refactored repeatedly and some obvious features not being planned for. The result was chaotic until the team realized there was a problem and members were able to communicate openly about what they wanted, so they introduced weekly design meetings until the design settled down.

Probably the most dangerous problem with new projects is that their newness rapidly fades. New projects often face immense pressure in that they need to produce a feature-complete project in as short a timeframe as possible. If there are established competitors, this can be an uphill battle. There are going to be more valleys than peaks, and a great deal of persistence and discipline is going to be required to stick with and refine the practices when the temptation is going to be to just crank out the features without considering what type of quality tradeoffs need to be made.

Some Other Ideas

Every project and situation is going to be different, so it is impossible to provide a step-by-step solution to your problem. I've tried to outline some of the common approaches I've used or seen applied to various situations, particularly when dealing with a legacy product that was not developed using sustainable techniques.

Identify Key Architecture Battles

Do an architectural analysis, where you identify things such as poor structure and areas with a large number of defects. Every time you modify these sections of code, even if only for a minor change, consider doing some refactoring work in addition to just making the changes, even if this means setting aside extra time to make the changes. Be sure to add tests at least for the new code, and if you can, identify the key interfaces and add tests for them.

In your iteration planning sessions, write up some cards for the refactoring work. Users, product managers, and managers are in my experience very supportive of refactoring work if they are involved in the process of helping to set overall priorities and understand, at least at a high level, the purpose of the refactoring work. The visibility that this gives to the architecture of the product is good for the entire team, while at the same time ensuring that architectural issues are weighed against the feature work that users are demanding.

Get Your Defects Under Control

Hopefully, you should now be convinced that defect backlogs are a bad thing. Introduce some visible metrics, and possibly an ambitious goal such as HP's "10x reduction goal" [Grady 1997] to get people focused on the problem. Then, work hard toward a culture built around defect prevention and working software.

Collaboration with Users

For many organizations, one of the most difficult steps in introducing agile development is getting timely feedback from users. This is an ideal problem for senior management in the company to get involved with, to set up the necessary user contacts and also to get everyone in the organization focused on the need for greater user contact.

Training

Training is a crucial part of moving from an unsustainable to sustainable development culture. Training needs to be considered for the entire team, ideally at the same time. In the early stages, using an external source (consultant or training organization) for training is usually required, because even if someone inside the company says the same things as the consultant, the consultant will often be listened to more, simply because he or she is from outside. However, once the initial training is complete, it is highly desirable to set up an internal training program, where people inside the company are given the opportunity to train others on topics they are knowledgeable in.

Group Refactoring Exercises

An unorthodox idea that I've seen work is a competitive refactoring exercise. Pick a piece of code that has many broken windows in it. Then, get a bunch of people together in a conference room and do a pair programming exercise to refactor the code. Consider pairing people together who don't work together too much. Use a projector to review the solutions that each pair came up with during the day and discuss the pros and cons of each. Optionally, an award could be given for the solution the group likes the best. This exercise is time-consuming, but it helps everyone understand the difference between good code and bad, and the result can often be applied in the live code the next day. Also, the discussions are valuable for everyone, and the whole process can be fun with an underlying thread of competition.

The Work Environment

One factor that is often overlooked when introducing change is the impact of the physical space the team works in. If you possibly can, change the physical space that the team operates in to facilitate collaboration and reduce unnecessary interruptions. Sometimes, simple changes can make huge differences in terms of productivity, and the highly collaborative nature of agile development demands a work environment that does not inhibit collaboration and free communication. Too many organizations are *penny wise, pound foolish* and skimp on equipment that will increase productivity simply because the equipment is considered too expensive. Here are some ideas to consider:

- Build a project room for the team or convert a meeting room into a project room. Cover the walls of the room with whiteboards and corkboards, and think of this space as the location where anyone can go to get an immediate idea of the progress of the project. The Apple II project, for example, had a *war room* that gave every member of the company instant insight into the project [Lynn and Reilly 2002].
- Make sure there are lots of whiteboards readily available and install a projector so the team can hold productive team code and architecture reviews. Magnetic whiteboards are also an ideal place to keep the index cards for iteration and release planning.
- Do people who run automated tests have fast computers? Computers are so inexpensive now that there should be no excuse to not ensuring that people have adequate computing power readily available.
- Do you need to buy dedicated computers for running automated tests?
- Do you use the right tools for your project?
- Are you using a good version control system?
- Are there SDKs, compilers, or development environments that would make your team more efficient?
- If the desks available to the team inhibit collaboration through having partitions that are too high or are not large enough for pair programming, find a way to buy some new furniture that removes these problems.

A Final Word

Sustainability and agility are more important than consistency.

If you have multiple teams working together or on multiple projects, it's more important that they have the same mindset than that they employ the exact same set of practices in exactly the same way. All that needs to be fostered is a free exchange of ideas between teams and a willingness to continually try out and discard ideas. This is far more fun, rewarding, and empowering than dictating practices!

Change Examples

I can't stand the status quo and prefer flexibility over any other mode of work. I try to always find better ways to do things and new ways to think about problems. I do this because I thrive on learning; my first priority is getting things done, and I prefer to get things done in the most efficient manner possible. I also like the element of surprise and producing an unexpected result or an unexpected analysis. Hence, I have been involved in many change efforts in my career at the personal, team, and organization levels. Not all have been successful, of course, but I've been fortunate that most of them have.

In this section I'll describe two successful changes. The first was the introduction of a controversial practice into a small development team, and the other was the introduction of agile development into a relatively large (approximately 200 people) mature software organization. I think they're both good examples of leadership and creating positive lasting change.

The Introduction of a Controversial Practice

The small-scale change was the introduction of the root-cause analysis practice I've described several times earlier in this book. At this time, I was a programmer working in a small and highly motivated team. We had a lot of good practices, and we thought we were doing pretty well. When our team leader first introduced the idea to the team of meeting once a week to review all our bugs, we resisted with all the predictable excuses: that it would take too much time, that the return on investment wouldn't be there, etc. But our team leader had some bug history data that convinced us enough to try it out for several months.

As predicted, the first few meetings were painful and took too long. However, I think it clicked for us after about a month when we realized that our drive to fix defects *properly* before the next meeting was paying dividends in increased quality. Around that time, we also developed an unproven belief that if we stuck with it, our overall productivity would increase. It took a few more months, but eventually we did reach the point where we were driven to reduce our defects through prevention (we got truly serious about automated testing), we always had a working product, and we held each other to increasingly high standards. Our productivity did increase, and we were able to add more features and deal with more complexity in a team that was constant in size.

In this case, our team leader deserves the credit for helping us take the initial leap and then essentially getting out of the way as we built on the early successes. I also acknowledge him for not taking any of the credit for the success of this change, although he certainly deserved it. For that team at that particular time, this was *the* right change that on hindsight took us from being a good (above average) to a great team. I was a member of that team as a programmer and team leader, and I am extremely proud of what we were able to accomplish.

Introducing Agile Development Into a Mature Software Organization

A few years ago the company I worked for closed down the office I worked at. The team I described in the previous example was dispersed, and we each went off and found different jobs. I joined a smaller company (approximately 400 people, about half of which are in product development) with a completely different software development culture. Its approach to software development was mostly the waterfall method, and it had been used and evolved for over a decade. I was there for about a year, left, and then came back because of the bright people, products, challenging problems, and amazing customers. When I came back, I was promoted into a new position where part of my mandate consisted of technology strategy, software architecture, and software development processes. Attention was needed in all three areas, but I believe that often process changes have the highest return, so that is where I decided to focus initially.

There was a general recognition that the software development processes were not what they should be. Some people were experimenting with different methods, but not with any noticeable success overall. There had been a few attempts to introduce new processes, but they had all failed. I spent a bit of time looking at each one and talking to the people who had been involved. The one attempt that left the biggest impression on me was one where the proposed process was meticulously documented with diagrams and loads of text. It was essentially a proposal to add more bureaucracy, with mandatory documents, sign-offs, and decision-making groups. Nobody really bought into it, for obvious reasons.

I was working with a woman from our HR group, and we decided that we wanted to bring in outside training and focus initially on project management. We started by obtaining an approved budget for some project management training. We spent a few weeks talking to consultants and various training groups. All but one of the groups we spoke to offered what I'll call traditional training in waterfall methods: Gantt charts, PERT charts, project tracking, etc. The one exception was Jim Highsmith. At the time, I had been reading anything I could get my hands on related to software development and development processes, from the CMM to agile. The books that had gotten me the most excited were the Extreme Programming books [Beck 2004] [Auer and Miller 2001] [Jeffries et al 2000], Jim's Adaptive Software Development [Highsmith 1999] book, and the Scrum book [Schwaber and Beedle 2001].

Initially, I wasn't content with any of the groups we spoke to about training. The traditional project management groups made me uncomfortable because, based on my previous work experience, I had minimal confidence that what they taught worked, except perhaps for building bridges. I was intrigued by agile development but didn't feel that any of the methods I had read about were complete. However, I realized that what really resonated with me about agile development were its principles (see www .agilemanifesto.org) and I was able to connect most of these principles to my previous job. We had a really good talk with Jim Highsmith, and he agreed to tailor a course for us that provided a balanced view across what I viewed at the time as project management and technical practices, with practices combined from ASD, XP, and Scrum.

Once we communicated our decision to provide agile development training, we encountered resistance. Mostly it was because at the time agile was new and viewed as largely untried. We were able to convince most people that the worst that could happen from such a course would be that people would have a few new ideas and skills to take away. Luckily, my boss and the majority of my peers were supportive. There was, however, one executive who was openly hostile to the idea and thought it was a waste of money and time. I spent an afternoon with him and outlined my arguments against the traditional methods (some are in the Introduction) and described my experience from my previous job. In the end, we agreed to disagree but, to his credit, he converted more to skepticism and a "wait-and-see" attitude. That experience prompted a phone call to Jim Highsmith, where we outlined a short course for the directors and select executives to introduce them to agile development and to give them a chance to ask detailed questions.

The next step was the actual training course. Our budget allowed us to initially run two 2-day courses plus a 2-hour course for directors and executives. We spent a fair bit of time identifying key people to get into the course (leaders at all levels), ensuring that we had a cross-section of all the various functions (team leaders, software developers, QA people, documentation writers, usability specialists, product managers, etc.) within our department, that the courses had a blend of vocal and quiet people, and that the skeptics were balanced by those we felt had a more open mind. Then we issued invitations and followed up if people didn't respond. A few people said no, but luckily we had a long list.

We held a kickoff prior to the first training session where we got all the course attendees together the day before the first course for 30 minutes. We had arranged for one of the executives to be there to give a short talk, but this person had to travel at the last minute, so it was left to me. I scribbled down some notes, rehearsed beforehand, and then spent some time "on my soapbox." Generally, I enjoy speaking in public, but I was very nervous that day because I knew this was a risk, and it was on me. I tried to *speak from the heart* and described my perspective on where we were and where we could be. For me, that little talk is when the change started.

The training courses went extremely well and the majority of the responses were positive. One of the reasons they went well is that quite a few people had been experimenting with approaches that were agile in spirit, but what had been lacking, perhaps, was the discipline, a framework, and a broader set of tried-and-true practices.

The next step was followup. One thing I always worry about with training courses is that it's easy for people to get enthused during the course, but the moment they get back to their desks and are confronted with their e-mail, voice mail, feature lists, bug backlog, etc. that reality can quickly overwhelm them. Later, they'll say they never had a chance to try out any of the new ideas. I also worry about situations where a select few people attend a course, come back enthusiastic, and then are beaten down by the pessimism of those who didn't attend the course. Therefore, as a followup, I decided to form an agile guiding council that consisted of the more enthusiastic course participants. The purpose of the group was to get as many people as possible as quickly as possible involved in leading the change and deciding what our next steps were.

The people in the guiding council are the ones who really made the change happen. We met weekly for the first year, then bi-weekly, and then sporadically for about another year after that. The council decided to bring in more training, so we got some more budget approved. This round of training would be a few one-day courses taught by Jim Highsmith and also some technical training that we thought should focus on test-first development, simple design, and refactoring. The council worked in subteams that did things like creating a vision statement and some nifty posters and sourcing and organizing the training. We also spent a lot of time talking about next steps, challenges, and successes. For the technical training, we chose Object Mentor, which eventually also ran some other courses for us. Jim Highsmith also visited us for a day once a month or so to talk to various people and groups. He definitely helped lend credibility to the initiative, because he could speak from his experiences at other companies.

Our first real success came about two months after the initial training. One of the team leaders had left the course and essentially thought "Hmm, that was interesting. I wonder if the company is going to do anything about it?" Then, through his participation in the council and with some encouragement from his peers on the council, he decided to try it out with his team. His team was enthusiastic about the Extreme Programming books, so members built out a quick project with test-first development, etc. The quality was amazing as was the speed that the results were achieved. It definitely turned some heads and got more people interested.

Shortly after the first success, the technical training started paying dividends. Some of the programmers had been adding unit tests to their new code, and as these tests started failing when other programmers modified the code, more people started noticing. The interesting thing is that our products prior to the training did have some automated tests. We had a unit test framework, for example, but it was only used by a few individuals and only sporadically. One of my favorite stories is that we had what were essentially system-level automated tests for one of our products. But everyone ignored the tests because they always failed, and they hadn't been updated in a long time. One day, one of the programmers called a meeting with all the team leaders for the product and, in a very nice way, outlined why the tests should be taken seriously! It was a turning point for that project.

There have been many interesting lessons learned to date. For example, we didn't really understand the importance of the physical workspace to agile development. Pair programming turned out to be impossible on most of our desks because they are too small for two people to sit side by side. For the curious, we don't mandate pair programming, and most of the people who do pair up only do so for an hour or two at a time. Another thing that was lacking was enough whiteboards. I'll never forget one day when I received an e-mail saying that we would have to erase the whiteboards when customers were touring the building so they wouldn't see anything confidential. My reply was a short NO, and luckily I managed to convince people that productivity was more important than customers seeing our building!

A few years later, I can safely say we have achieved lasting change. It isn't uniform across all teams, because there is still a divide between our new products developed since agile was introduced and those that existed before. We have rapidly developed one amazing new product, and we're developing other new products using the same methods. We have built up several new areas now with new desks, and we have happily converted many of our former formal sit-down meeting rooms into agile project rooms where the walls are plastered with magnetic whiteboards and corkboards. As a result, a number of large tables have been relegated to the basement to collect dust so we can stand up and move around.

The challenges for our existing projects have been quite large. The teams have adopted as many agile practices as they can, and they've added many new automated tests. But the amount of code that isn't covered by automated tests is quite large, and in many cases not enough attention was paid in the past to issues such as code duplication and design, so the teams are still paying off accumulated technical debt. Still, huge strides have been made and the teams are motivated to continually improve. I hope that eventually we can close the gap with our other teams.

Summary

Implementing sustainable development in most organizations is going to require a change in the development culture. This chapter is an introduction to some techniques that can be used while outlining change factors and enablers that must be thought of. Achieving a culture change is hard and requires more effort and persistence than most people anticipate. Hence, it is important to consider what you want to achieve and how you are going to achieve it.

Practice Summary

This appendix contains a summary of all the principles and practices outlined in this book. The main purpose of this appendix is to help understand how critical each of the practices described in this book is to overall success and to help get started on a new project. In particular, I would like to highlight the *keystone practices*, which are the practices that make the largest contribution toward achieving the overall principles or mindset for sustainable development.

Keystone Species in a Natural Ecosystem

One of my favorite books in the area of natural biology is called *Krakatau: The Destruction and Reassembly of an Island Ecosystem* [Thornton 1996]. On August 27, 1883, the island of Krakatau was virtually obliterated by a volcanic explosion. The island was literally reduced to a lifeless rock. This book is about Dr. Ian Thornton's visits over many years to the island and his observations as the island slowly and gradually came back to life from virtually nothing to a thriving and complete ecosystem.

One aspect of his analysis that I find fascinating is his identification of *keystone species*. These are the species of plants and animals that, if they disappeared, would cause the entire ecosystem to apart, or, if they were absent, then the ecosystem would not develop as it should. In the case of Krakatau, one of these species was the fig tree. It is fascinating to read how, once the fig tree became established on the island, the pace of change on the island accelerated.

I think the notion of a keystone species in an ecosystem carries over to the idea of keystone practices for sustainable software development. As I've outlined throughout this book, the complexity of the ecosystem that software inhabits dictates a mindset or principles that lead to success in both the short and long term. And critical to the desired mindset are a set of practices that act as keystones for the approach to software development. Hence, while it is inevitable that practices change over time and that the exact set of practices employed is going to depend on the team and the circumstances of its project, certain practices are going to change more than others, while others form the foundation that all the other practices are built around. If it were possible to start from a clean slate (like Krakatau), then given the mindset required for sustainability as a starting condition, some practices are going to be obvious starting points.

Keystone practices are identified with the icon:

Working Product

1. No "Broken Windows"	Bad code should never be tolerated because one mess leads to another, and another, and another, . . .
2. Be Uncompromising about Defects	For sustainability, defect backlogs must be avoided at all costs, starting from the early days of a project.
3. "Barely Sufficient" Documentation	Although this practice is important, I've worked on teams that produced lots of documentation and still got a good product to market. As long as the focus is on producing a working product and not the documents, and as long as the majority of effort goes into the product and not the documents, then sustainability can still result.
4. Continuous Integration	Teams that delay integration are simply delaying the time when they will have to deal with the inevitable problems. The more often integration occurs, the faster problems are uncovered.
5. Nightly Builds	Having a nightly build that works is the first level of reassurance that the product is working.
6. Prototyping	Prototyping is a simple and effective way to reduce risk and better understand a problem before having to solve it *live*.
7. Don't Neglect Performance	Performance is one of those aspects of a product that can't be neglected for long. You can probably get by

	without paying attention to performance for a while but at some point you're going to have to invest in it.
8. Zero Tolerance for Memory and Resource Leaks	This is a keystone practice only if you are using a programming language where programmers are responsible for memory and resource management.
9. Coding Standards and Guidelines	How badly you need standards and guidelines is going to depend on the experience level of the team and the degree of similarity in the working habits of team members. Coding standards and guidelines can help many teams have useful discussions about good and bad code.
10. Adopt Standards (Concentrate on Your Value-Add)	You can reinvent the wheel and still complete a project, but you're still wasting effort. This is one of those mindsets that becomes more important with experience, as you learn to use what is available to you as long as it is good enough and stifle the temptation to build it yourself.
11. Internationalize From Day One	Many projects don't care about supporting multiple languages. However, for those projects that do, there are simple things you can do in the early days of the project that will save wasted effort later.
12. Isolate Platform Dependencies	If portability between platforms is a concern for your project, make sure you isolate the dependencies, preferably through platform-independent abstractions so that platform issues are not exposed to the majority of the code. If platform-specific code is strewn everywhere, then the code is harder to maintain and more error-prone, and this makes it hard to keep the product in a working state.

Defect Prevention

1. Ruthless Testing	⚿ Most projects rely too much on manual testing and having people perform repetitive tasks that should be automated and performed on a regular basis by computers.

2. Use Available Tools	There are tools available that, if used wisely, can boost productivity. Teams should use the tools that are available to them to help prevent problems while constantly being on the lookout for new tools.
3. Pair Programming and Code Reviews	This practice helps catch defects while increasing the understanding of team members in the code they are collectively working on. However, the danger is that these not get out of control, which happens if pair programming is mandated or code reviews are distributed too widely.
4. Lightweight Root-Cause Analysis	This can be an extremely valuable practice, although it can also get out of control. The team needs to carefully use this one.

Design Emphasis

1. Design Vision	Having a simple and easily understood design vision helps the team make daily design decisions that fit within the long-term goals of the project. Sustainability can be compromised if the team does not consider the mid to long term in their daily decisions.
2. Guiding Principles	Guiding principles reinforce the design vision and help the team keep principles that are important to sustainability in mind.
3. Simple Design	Simplicity is vital for sustainable development because simplicity tends to make software easier to modify and less brittle over time.
4. Refactoring	Continual disciplined refactoring, with an eye toward cleaning up code while maintaining the desired behavior, is important for sustainability because it allows the team to evolve its software with confidence.
5. Design Patterns	Design patterns are a tool that every developer should be aware of and understand when to use them and how to use them properly. At their best, they can save a great deal of effort. At their worst, they can contribute to making software overly complex and brittle.

6. Frequent Rapid Design Meetings	Collaboration about design, as frequently as possible, is where design starts. Having a forum to talk about good design and good code and not just problems helps everyone on the team.
7. Commitment to Re-Architecture	(Especially for large development efforts) A commitment to re-architecture is a keystone practice on projects that involve large teams and large amounts of code that must change over a number of years. On these larger projects, being willing to make difficult decisions to re-architect portions of the system can make the difference between sustainability and unsustainability.
8. Design for Reuse	(Especially for large development efforts) Designing for reuse is a keystone practice on projects that involve large teams and large amounts of code that change over a number of years. This is because the costs of duplicated effort are magnified the greater the effort, not only in initial design and development time but also in ongoing maintenance as changes are made that must be carefully made in multiple places.

Continual Refinement

1. Iterative Development	Iterative development is a key underpinning of sustainable development. By breaking the project down into small manageable chunks of time, the team is able to reduce risk, continually monitor its progress, and make course corrections as required—even if no changes are ever made to the scheduled features.
2. Release Planning	(For most projects) Release planning is an important aspect of projects that are going to take more than some number of months or are released to customers on a regular basis. For these projects, having a clear idea of what is going to be in a release contributes to sustainability because it helps teams plan architectural changes

	that support the release and that make future change easier.
3. Daily Standup Meetings	(Especially for small teams) Some form of daily collaboration is important for people to work effectively together. And having a team that works well together is important for sustainability. Daily standup meetings work best in small teams where team members are all in the same location and meet face-to-face every day. In large teams, daily collaboration is still required, but it is difficult to achieve. This is where team members should consider experimenting with every means at their disposal to find something that will work for them.
4. Retrospectives	 Frequent lightweight retrospectives are crucial to help teams learn and continually improve what they are doing and how they are working. Sustainability is virtually impossible without this continual learning and improvement.
5. Coaching and Team Development	 Coaching is finding ways to bring out the best in people and getting them to work together without telling them what to do and how to do it. Both coaching and team development (through professional development and having some understanding of the business) are vital for sustainable development, because people need to perform at their best.
6. Make Key Metrics Visible	Measuring the key metrics for a project and making them visible gives teams a simple and visual means of understanding how they are doing. The dangers of metrics are that they become the focal point of efforts to the exclusion of all else and also that there are too many metrics to be useful.

Appendix 2

Extreme Programming and Sustainable Software Development

The purpose of this appendix is to describe the strengths and weaknesses of Extreme Programming (XP) because XP is the most visible of the agile methods. The message of this appendix should be that XP is good, but that when it comes to achieving sustainable development, XP's values and practices are a good start but are not sufficient.

The Four Values of XP

1. **Communication.**
   Clear and effective communication is required from customers (to communicate their needs), developers (to describe what is possible), and managers (to help set expectations) to make an effective project.

2. **Simplicity.**

A product should only be as complex as is actually required for the problem at hand. Overly complex products have many subtle and unnecessary problems.

3. **Feedback.**

Proper feedback stops problems as early as possible in the development process.

4. **Courage.**

The team must have the courage to take risks and try new ideas and approaches. Timely feedback will highlight problems as early as possible.

XP's Twelve Practices

XP's twelve practices are derived from the four values.

1. **Test Driven Development.**

Unit tests written before and during coding allow rapid change by providing confidence that errors aren't creeping into the product.

2. **Small Releases.**

Small releases help ensure that the developers and customers are able to provide each other with continuous feedback.

3. **Refactoring.**

Refactoring allows the design to be continually enhanced and simplified over time by reducing redundancy and complexity.

4. **Simple Design.**

Reducing complexity is just as important as coding.

5. **Planning Game.**

Only plan enough to get started and refine the plan after every release.

6. **Pair Programming.**

All production code is written by two people collaborating at the keyboard. This enables collective code ownership and helps to catch coding problems as early as possible.

7. **Onsite Customer.**

An onsite customer ensures that feedback is nearly instantaneous so no time is wasted waiting.

8. **System Metaphor.**

   A common real-world metaphor that is understood by customers, developers, and managers is used for elements of the project.

9. **Collective Code Ownership.**

   Collective code ownership helps ensure that no one team member is the critical path or sole repository of knowledge on a particular section of code.

10. **Continuous Integration.**

    Changes are placed into the shared version control system as early and often as possible so that every developer is working from the latest version of the software. This helps to ensure that problems are caught as early as possible.

11. **Coding Conventions.**

    Consistent coding conventions aid communication within the team and reduce the amount of time required to learn a new section of code.

12. **Sustainable Pace.**

    Work at a consistent pace so that consistent and accurate estimates can be made. Use a 40-hour work week to ensure there is also a balance between home and work.

The Strengths of XP

The main strength of XP is that it is designed to appeal directly to software developers. The XP practices, and the emphasis on coaching and self-organized teams are most likely a reaction to software development cultures that stress project management and bureaucracy as a means to achieve successful projects. XP is likely also a reaction to bad managers who tell teams what to do, when, and how to do it.

XP has introduced a healthy debate within the software industry. Traditional engineering methods place decision-making power primarily in the hands of managers through bureaucracy, tracking plans, unnecessary milestones, and documentation as a tracked deliverable. XP counters bureaucracy by placing the decision-making power in the hands of the software development team and the software's users. Instead, by emphasizing value to customers through working software not documentation, practices that emphasize technical excellence, collaboration between developers, and direct customer contact, XP is steering the industry more toward producing high-quality and high-value results for customers, which is exactly where the emphasis should be.

XP **is** Extreme

One of the appeals of XP is that it is extreme, especially compared to traditional software development practices. Pair programming, test-driven development, refactoring, the planning game, etc. are all completely out of the normal realm of experience for traditional software teams. As a result, XP has received a lot of attention and has gotten people to think and question their development methods. The resulting debates have been good for the software industry.

Technical Excellence

XP's focus on technical excellence is particularly important. Although it's hard to identify core practices, a case could be made that they are simple design, refactoring, and test-driven development. Each of these practices is simple yet powerful and helps to emphasize achieving results as quickly as possible so that users can provide feedback and changes made in response to the user comments. Likewise, continuous integration helps teams focus on keeping their software integrated and working through unit tests and the goal of frequent and small releases.

Collaboration

There is no doubt that XP gets teams working together, intimately. Tight collaboration within teams is a vital aspect of success, and by emphasizing pair programming, collective ownership, self-organizing teams, and having an on-site customer focuses teams on collaborating. The result is exhilarating and fun for those involved, and the results are often phenomenal. Greater collaboration helps to ensure that common problems such as duplicated code and effort, unmaintainable code, and independently developed modules unable to integrate with each other. The integration problem is particularly acute; I have seen projects where two developers working in the same cubicle produce modules that can't be integrated, even when integration was a key design issue!

XP's collaborative practices help to avoid the *hero syndrome*. We all know the heroes; they're the ones who work long hours to get the critical features into the software. At many companies, they're rewarded by the company for doing so, and there is a general recognition that the company would be in deep trouble if they left. My experience with heroes (and I will confess that in my first job in industry I was one of them) is that they either leave behind a swath of destruction in the code, or they definitely leave behind code that can't be maintained by anyone else because nobody else knows the code the way they do. While it is true that the best programmers do produce more [Demarco and Lister 1999], often considerably more, there is still plenty of room through collaboration to keep the output of the best programmers high while making the *entire team* into the heroes through high-value and high-quality results.

Customer Collaboration

The most important aspect of XP's collaborative practices is the emphasis on collaboration with customers. Because customers are involved in the planning of iterations and prioritization, and because there are regular releases of software to customers, the team is able to get timely feedback that helps to ensure team members are always doing what is most important to the customer. Thus, XP maximizes value to the customer while minimizing the amount of effort required to create that value through decreasing effort wasted on nonessential work.

The Weaknesses of XP

Many of the weaknesses of XP stem from the fact that it is often presented in a semi-religious, almost cult-like way. This is the view that in order to practice XP, you need to utilize all the practices and stick with them to the letter, with no alternative if you can't use them or want to add to them. There are some in the XP community who recognize this problem, so hopefully this view will moderate over time.

XP is also subject to problems of interpretation. People who read the XP books or speak to XP teams can easily misinterpret the practices, overzealously apply them, and then decide that since one or two of the practices don't work, therefore XP doesn't, when in fact the XP mindset does work, and the XP practices around test-first development, refactoring, and simple design in particular are absolutely brilliant. People who dismiss XP as a whole are missing out on some valuable practices. Unfortunately, you don't have to look too hard on the Internet to find articles that reflect the failed XP experience.

XP Targets Software Developers, and Nobody Else

XP is too narrowly targeted at software developers. Successful software products are developed by teams, and this is stating the obvious, but teams include more than just software developers. Documentation, business people, Quality Assurance (QA), and usability are glaring omissions. Often, these other functions use practices that are incompatible with XP and then struggle with experimental practices, or because there is so much emphasis on the software these other functions are minimized –[md] to the possible peril of the project.

The role of the manager is particularly abused in XP. I know quite a few managers who have read *Extreme Programming Explained* [Beck 2004] and been turned off on the whole thing because managers are cast in the role of the bad guy. While it can't be disputed that some managers *are* the bad guys, I believe that most managers want success and are a part of that success, not a hindrance to it. Perhaps the label *manager* is the problem. XP disdains bureaucrats (who tell what to do, when, and how) and while it is true that bureaucrats are not desired, leaders who know how to set up a collaborative, empowering environment are *definitely* required. Some people call this role the *coach*, and while that does capture the essence of this style of leadership, I believe that coaching is just one attribute of a successful leader.

Project Management

XP describes a project planning paradigm that is useful for a small team of software developers. Given XP's focus on software developers, this shouldn't be a surprise, nor should it be viewed as particularly bad because the practices are useful for some teams. However, the lack of a more rigorous attention on project management has led agile practitioners to propose hybrid agile techniques such as Scrum with XP [Schwaber and Beedle 2001] or ASD with XP [Highsmith 1999] and why Jim Highsmith, for example, wrote his excellent book *Agile Project Management* [Highsmith 2004a].

Scalability

XP was developed for the C3 project for Chrysler. It featured a small project team with a single customer. The XP practices alone are hard to scale to larger teams because (among many things) they do not offer any solutions to collaboration between teams, or as mentioned above, do not address any of the issues faced by non-software developers in the team.

Another aspect of scalability is a result of the fact that XP is primarily targeted at software developers. Because XP typically starts in software teams, change is attempted in a purely bottom-up way that can be transferred to other software teams but not through an entire organization without extra practices.

Pair Programming

Pair programming is presented as something that software developers absolutely must do. Yet, pair programming is **hard**: Either you are typing or you are watching someone else type, often poorly or slowly. The reader of the XP books is left with the impression that developers should pair program all day, every day. While pair programming can be very useful and productive, its use should be limited to what the people on the team are comfortable with. It certainly shouldn't be mandated.

What gets lost in the pair programming debate is that the intent of pair programming is to encourage *collaboration* between developers and to ensure that problems are caught as the code is typed. Essentially, by forcing pair programming, you force developers to collaborate with each other with the goal of building a team that collaborates by default, and in person not through e-mail or some other contrived means. There are other ways to achieve this same level of collaboration, and it's much healthier to encourage a range of collaborative practices than to mandate a single one.

The 40-Hour Week

The other practice that is often overzealously applied is the 40-hour work-week. I have read articles where XP teams were criticized because, instead of pushing to get a product out the door, they have insisted on working no overtime, and hence lack any sense of urgency. I also have spoken to people who claim to be using XP but work 80-hour weeks on a regular basis, which also isn't good.

The purpose of the 40-hour workweek is to get teams to work hours that allow them to stay sane and have a life outside work over the long term, measured in many months to years. This sense of balance is important to maintain a sustainable pace of development. The reality is that extra hours are going to be required on occasion, so the emphasis should be on the work/life balance over the mid to long term with a rational average number of hours per week worked. Reasonable working hours and avoiding burnout are a *result* of the focus on sustainable development, not *the* focus. Thus, sustainable development requires principles and practices that target sustainability and increasing capability over time.

The On-Site Customer

On-site customers are great if you can get them, or if you can work on your customer site where your customer is readily available. But what if your product has thousands of customers? Tens of thousands? Hundreds of thousands? What if your product sells to customers in many diverse vertical market segments, where each market has unique requirements? The bottom line is that in many cases it is impossible to have a true on-site customer. Many teams who try XP fail because they are unable to get over this hurdle, because XP and all the agile development techniques work best when there is a timely feedback loop between the customer and development team. Unfortunately, this is a rich enough topic for another book, but there are alternatives that are different from having an on-site customer but equally as useful. Just so you aren't left hanging, here are a few ideas:

- Learn about the field of usability or, even better, hire a usability expert or team. Usability professionals have a rich and diverse number of ways to test software with users and get the required feedback that agile teams need.
- Use the Internet to ship your software on a regular basis (daily or weekly) and get feedback from your customers so they can provide you with instant feedback and you can solve their problems in an optimal time. More on this in Chapter 4 on Working Software.
- Have a customer representative on your team. This person is a user of the product who spends a great deal of his or her time talking to and working with customers on real problems. These representatives funnel the feedback from customers into the team and give team members the feedback they need when they need it.

Self-Organization and Leadership

Many teams get carried away with self-organization and forget that there are often situations where people with specific roles are required. For example, it almost always makes sense to have a project leader to deal with the daily coordination and management of the project. Good project leaders (or coaches) are able to nudge teams forward, while helping them to make the right decisions and know the right decision when they see it. Pure democracy doesn't always work, and sometimes somebody needs to step forward and make a tough decision where there is no clear consensus, simply in the interest of keeping the project moving forward.

A related topic is that there is a general trend to shy away from the term leadership in XP. As explained in Chapter 8, leadership is a critical success factor in successful projects and is required at all levels of an organization.

Leadership is not a top-down thing. It is required at all levels, and effective leaders lead their peers and their bosses, too.

Simple Design

In XP, simple design means only designing what you need to know immediately. As explained in Chapter 6, the problem with this definition is that in many teams this leads to an unhealthy desire to avoid having overall guidelines and design scheme.

Common Misconceptions of Extreme Programming

Another weakness of XP is that there are some common misconceptions in circulation. I think these are a result of people who read the XP books and try to implement the practices without understanding the principles behind XP.

"No Design"

Unfortunately, there are teams who have adopted XP because they believe it frees them from having to do design. XP is not a license to hack. Just because the emphasis is on working software and simple design does not remove the need to do design (see Chapter 6). No doubt these teams live in an environment where the design burden in terms of undue ceremony and documentation is high, but swinging the pendulum to the complete other extreme is not the correct response either.

Good software developers always think about a problem and plan their approach before they write any code. The difference is that in XP, instead of focusing on a detailed design document as the key output of the design process, the most important attribute is the software and the process you go through to produce the design.

"No Discipline"

Many people feel that XP teams are not disciplined. Actually, XP requires a great deal of discipline. The misunderstanding comes in through the definition of discipline. Typically, those who think XP teams are not disciplined think of discipline as *process compliant,* where the process dictates the production of documents in a carefully staged order of analysis then coding. These people use the absence of the documents created in traditional development (e.g., requirements documents, design documents) as evidence that agile teams are undisciplined. There are also feelings of discomfort that agile teams do not put any effort into understanding user requirements or do not do design, when in fact they do. The difference is that with agile approaches, the emphasis is on the software, not documents, and making a decision as late as possible.

Discipline is more than just documents or rules; it is a function of the people in the team. Agile development provides a simple model that can be used to give a project a regular heartbeat with a constant understanding of progress and learning. It is up to the people in the teams to take advantage of the information they have. This is really no different than in traditional development: Discipline is up to the people on the team and not an attribute of the methodology.

Other Agile Development Methods

Many people have only heard of XP or think that agile development *is* XP. This is a pity, because there are other agile methods that have a lot to offer. In an environment where a team emphasizes agility and continual improvement in capability through regular retrospectives and experimentation with methods, the other agile methods are an ideal source of ideas and practices. My favorites are:

- Adaptive Software Development [Highsmith 1999] and Agile Project Management [Highsmith 2004a]
- Lean Development [Poppendieck and Poppendieck 2003]. Lean development is inspired by lean manufacturing [Womack and Jones 1996].
- Feature-Driven Development [Palmer and Felsing 2002].

- Crystal [Cockburn 2001] [Cockburn 2004].
- SCRUM [Schwaber and Beedle 2001].
- Dynamic Systems Development Method (DSDM) [Stapleton 2003]. DSDM introduces a healthy business focus to agile techniques.
- Agile Development Ecosystems [Highsmith 2002] contains a good summary of agile development and agile methods.

Summary

Don't be deceived by the fact that there is more text in this appendix dedicated to the weaknesses of XP than to its strengths. The strengths more than balance out the weaknesses, and as with *any* software development method, it is easy to poke holes in the implementation. The practices of XP are an excellent place to start, but XP should not be viewed as a complete methodology.

The most critical element that is missing with XP is the notion of continual learning and improvement in the methods used by the team. Every team is different because it's made up of different people and faces a different ecosystem. Hence, teams need to place an emphasis on continual improvement of their methods through regular retrospectives and methodology changes that are consistent with the principles (mindset) of sustainable development. This gives them a more healthy balance between software and non-software and should encourage them to continually look for new ideas. If your team is using XP, I highly recommend that you try out new practices as required while staying true to the values. XP unfortunately gets too much attention in the software community. This is both good and bad: good in the sense that XP has caused a large number of developers to question the traditional methods of software development, and bad in the sense that there is more to agile development than XP. There are quite a few other agile methods, and each offers different agile practices or viewpoints that should be consulted and incorporated as a team continually looks for new sources of ideas and inspiration.

Sustainable Software Development and the CMM

The misconception among many commercial software developers is that process discipline in software development (such as the CMM) is incompatible with fast-moving development processes such as XP. A similar misconception among many process-oriented people—CMM or otherwise—is that developing software quickly is tantamount to chaos. If these two views persist, they will keep excellent development teams from realizing the benefits of structured process improvement, and likewise keep larger organizations from looking at alternative development methods. [Glazer 2001]

The Capability Maturity Model (CMM) was developed by the Software Engineering Institute as a way to describe the maturity of a software organization's development practices. People who practice agile development view the CMM as being the opposite of agile: ponderous, cumbersome, and antiquated. Process-oriented people look upon agile methods as being undisciplined and chaotic. However, from the standpoint of sustainable development, there is actually a great deal to learn from and draw on from both agile development and the CMM. As pointed out in the quote above, people who dismiss agile are missing the benefits of simple and powerful development methods, and people who dismiss the CMM are limiting their ability to implement organizational process improvements. In this Appendix, I will briefly describe the CMM and then show how the CMM and agile development complement each other.

The Capability Maturity Model (CMM)

The Software CMM [Paulk et al 1993] is a five-level model that describes good engineering and management practices and prescribes improvement priorities for software organizations [Paulk 2001]. The intent of the CMM is to provide areas of focus (called Key Process Areas or KPAs) for software organizations that have proven in many software organizations to lead to excellence in software development. The Software Engineering Institute also provides standard guidelines for assessment, so that a third-party assessor can evaluate an organization and produce a report that outlines the maturity of the organization's processes. The combination of the CMM model and objective third-party assessments means that an organization can at any time have an understanding of its current capabilities plus the types of activities it must focus on to move to the next level. Hence, the CMM is intended to provide a general framework for planning and measuring the capability of a software organization. The CMM does not specify or mandate actual development processes, it merely specifies *what* to do in general terms.

The five maturity levels of the CMM and the KPAs associated with each level of maturity are shown in Table A3-1. CMM level 1 organizations are characterized by chaotic processes that require heroism to complete software projects. At the other extreme, CMM level 5 organizations have competence in all the KPAs, established processes, and are continually improving their processes.

Because the CMM does not specify the actual processes that should be used in software development, CMM 5 maturity does not necessarily equate with software quality or sustainability. It *usually* does, but that is more the result of the methods put in place by the people who designed the processes and their hard work. Also, in my experience at any large company, there is a great deal of variability in the quality of work between teams. Hence, CMM 5 is *not* a guarantee that the traditional *code-then-fix* method not used. I have worked with CMM 5 companies as subcontractors, and my experience is that while the majority of them produced excellent work, there were some groups that frankly shocked me with the poor quality of the work they produced.

Table A3-1. The Five Maturity Levels of the CMM and the KPAs Associated with Each Level of Maturity

Level	Focus	Key Process Areas
5 Optimizing	*Continual process improvement*	Defect Prevention Technology Change Management Process Change Management
4 Managed	*Product and process quality*	Quantitative Process Management Software Quality Management
3 Defined	*Engineering processes and organizational support*	Organization Process Focus Organization Process Definition Training Program Integrated Software Management Software Product Engineering Intergroup Coordination Peer Reviews
2 Repeatable	*Project management processes*	Requirements Management Software Project Planning Software Project Tracking & Oversight Software Subcontract Management Software Quality Assurance Software Configuration Management
1 Initial	*Competent people and heroics*	

Agile Development and the CMM

Agile development and the CMM can co-exist. Since the CMM specifies the *what* (in terms of the KPAs) and is methodology neutral, agile development methods can be used as the method (the *how*) to achieve much of CMM process maturity. Also, if you've gotten this far in this book, it should be obvious that the claim that agile development does not require discipline is very much false. Agile development is hard work and requires a great deal of discipline.

The practices of extreme programming have been contrasted with the CMM KPAs in various articles [Glazer 2001] [Paulk 2001] [Bandaru 2004]. If you are interested, I highly recommend reading them. The conclusion reached by all these sources is that the extreme programming practices do offer a solution to most of the KPAs. Of the eighteen KPAs, six are largely addressed in XP, and five are partially addressed. In this book, I have consciously added practices such as configuration management, professional development, and business knowledge because they are implied in the agile literature, but required for sustainable development. As a bonus, they happen to also be called out as KPAs. Likewise, the principles of continual refinement and defect prevention turn out to be level 5 KPAs, and are thus of extremely high value to software organizations.

What I find particularly intriguing with agile development and the CMM is the role of the agile mindset in the implementation of development processes. As I have personally discovered, *an organization can only be as agile as its least agile part*. Furthermore, since software teams must by their nature be cross-functional, if one functional part of the team is not agile, then the entire team will feel the effects. Here are some examples that I have personally seen:

- Product management and/or engineering management that wants to completely specify all the features that make up the next software release before any code is written. Sometimes it is really hard for people to accept that they can't predict what the next release will contain, even if that release date is a year out or more. If these feature lists are followed religiously, there is no room for agility.
- A marketing department that needs a large amount of lead time to write the marketing material for the next release. This means it will be hard to add features that are important to users late in a release cycle, and this limits agility.
- A documentation group that is used to working on documentation after all the features are done. If it takes a long time to write the documentation, then documentation is going to continually lag development and slow it down.
- A software testing team that is heavily relied upon by developers to find defects (i.e., a defect detection culture). Invariably, the testing group will become a bottleneck and will also be frustrated by the poor quality of the product given to them to test.

- Bizarre manufacturing policies that dictate, for example, that physical CDs must be produced for all releases, that a minimum inventory must be maintained, and that every new release must involve new CDs for example, electronic distribution and the Internet are not utilized or are thought of as secondary to the CDs. Agile products must ship regularly; if each shipment costs money, it may be easier to question the frequent releases than to question the silly practices that cause the high costs . . .

Each of above examples illustrates the problem with process improvement in an organization. If you choose to become an agile organization, then agile can start in software teams, but it had better spread, or overall the positive effects of agile development will not be as noticeable as they should be. This is where the principles of agile development come in because they must be applied across the entire organization. The practices will largely differ depending on the function (i.e., software developers will have different practices than documentation people or marketing people), but the mindset must be similar to maximize overall agility.

The topic of an agile enterprise is one that could easily occupy a book of its own. As an exercise to interested readers, I would recommend that you read through the principles in the Agile Manifesto (www.agilemanifesto .org) and reflect on the role of each in all the functional areas of your software teams. In terms of the principles of sustainability outlined in this book and some of the select practices, I believe that there is a great deal of applicability to CMM maturity:

- Continual refinement in *how* the team works through frequent retrospectives and tuning of processes is a level 5 KPA.
- Having a working product every day, even if it is not functionally complete, makes Software Quality Management (a level 4 KPA) attainable. The goals of SQM are to plan the SQM goals (in this case: it works), make them measurable, and to quantify and manage the goals.
- Defect prevention is a level 5 KPA.
- The notion of minimal documentation applies to many of the KPAs. However, most notable is how it applies to Organization Process Definition (a level 3 KPA). There's nothing wrong with creating a diagram and short description of your agile process as is done in

[Highsmith 2004a] and accompanying that with a list of best practices and lessons learned. Such a document would be useful in a large organization, especially if it's continually updated and it's only as long as it needs to be. A 50-page document can often convey the same information as a 500-page document. Besides, in the agile way, what's wrong with leaving some things open to experimentation as long as teams are using the agile principles?

Summary

The CMM and agile development aren't opposites. There is value to understanding the CMM and applying it to an organization's process improvement initiatives, even if the organization wishes to be agile. The CMM outlines best practices that are not covered by agile development, such as the areas of management and process management, and these are vital to the overall organization. Agile development provides principles, or mindset, plus additional practices that are equally important to avoid a bureaucratic approach. Hence, the CMM and agile can coexist.

Recommended Reading

Chapters 1 and 2: Sustainable Software Development, Unsustainable Software Development

[Christensen 2003] Clayton M. Christensen, *The Innovator's Dilemma,* HarperBusiness, 2003.

[Christensen and Raynor 2003] Clayton M. Christensen and Raynor, Michael E., *The Innovator's Solution,* Harvard Business School Press, 2003.

> These two books should be considered classic business books. The innovator's dilemma is that there is a risk that if you listen exclusively to your customers, a new wave of technology will come along to put you out of business. These books point out the need for companies to find ways to disrupt themselves, no matter how painful.

[Collins 2001] Collins, Jim, *Good to Great,* HarperBusiness, 2001.

> This book is a business classic that describes the difference between good companies and great companies. No software companies are featured in the book, and perhaps that says something? There is much to learn from in this book, even if you are interested in a more limited topic such as the difference between good teams and great teams.

[Collins and Porras 2002] Collins, Jim, and Porras, Jerry I., *Built to Last: Successful Habits of Visionary Companies,* HarperBusiness, 2002.

> There are elements of this book that I like a great deal, and others that I find dated today. My feelings about this book are perhaps jaded by an experience at a former company where a great deal of effort was put into formulating the company vision and mission, but it didn't do one bit of good because of numerous bad decisions...

[Economist 2004] *Make it Simple: A Survey of Information Technology*, The Economist, October 2004.

> If you can find a copy of this article, it is well worth reading. The article discusses what the author feels to be the largest problem with technology today: the need for simplicity. It will be particularly interesting to read this article in a few years, since the article mentions some up-and-coming technologies, many of which are likely to fail or be unable to live up to the hype.

[Norman 1999] Norman, Donald A., *The Invisible Computer,* MIT Press, 1999.

> This is one of my favorite books on usability because it makes you think about simplicity. It describes the classic *Crossing the Chasm* [Moore 2002] problem in terms of usability and places usability on an equal footing in terms of importance with technology and marketing.

[Repenning and Sterman 2001] Repenning, Nelson P. and Sterman, John D., *Nobody Ever Gets Credit for Fixing Problems That Never Happened: Creating and Sustaining Process Improvement*, California Management Review, Vol. 43 No. 4, Summer 2001.

> I was thrilled when I first found this paper because even though it is a study of chemical manufacturing plants and has nothing to do with software development, it speaks to many of the issues faced by today's software organizations.

Chapter 3: The Principles of Sustainable Development

[Boehm and Turner 2004] Boehm, Barry and Turner, Richard, *Balancing Agility and Discipline,* Addison Wesley, 2004.

> In my opinion, this book should be titled *Balancing Agility and Ceremony.* This is because the mistaken impression that some people have drawn from the title is that *agility* is the opposite of *discipline.* And that is most emphatically incorrect. Once you get past that point, this is actually an excellent book that describes a model for understanding and contrasting various approaches to software development and the challenges faced by different software projects.

[Buckingham and Coffman 1999] Buckingham, Marcus and Coffman, Curt, *First, Break all the Rules,* Simon & Schuster, 1999.

> This is an excellent book that focuses on the difference between talents and skills. Skills can be learned, and, while some talents can be improved, they are largely born not made. The book contains a number of interesting chapters on topics such as helping people identify their talents and how to put people in positions where they can best utilize their talents.

[Demarco and Lister 1999] Demarco, Tom and Lister, Timothy, *Peopleware: Productive Projects and Teams,* 2nd Edition, Dorset House Publishing Company, 1999.

> This is a software development classic and is highly recommended.

[Lundin et al 2000] Lundin, Stephen C., Paul, Harry, and Christensen, John, *Fish! A Remarkable Way to Improve Morale and Boost Results,* Hyperion, 2000.

> This book takes only a few minutes to read and it is time well spent. The main theme of the book is that you can't always choose what you work on, but you *can* choose how you do it. The difference is critical, and the more people who understand this message, the better the chance that the modern workplace could be transformed from drudgery to fun and inspiring.

[Lynn and Reilly 2002] Lynn, Gary S., Reilly, Richard P., *Blockbusters: The Five Keys to Developing GREAT New Products,* HarperBusiness, 2002.

Although this book is not about sustainable development or even software development, it is a good book about innovative product development. There are quite a few parallels between the methods described in this book and agile development methods: particularly about the need for iterative development (which the authors call *lickety-stick innovation*), collaboration, and physical spaces that enhance collaboration and communication.

Chapter 4: Working Product

[Ambler and Jeffries 2002] Ambler, Scott W., Jeffries, Ron, *Agile Modeling,* Wiley, 2002.

This is the best book I've seen on the topic of lightweight documentation. It is packed with ideas on how to capture requirements, specifications, design, etc.

[Beck 2004] Beck, Kent, *Extreme Programming Explained,* 2nd Edition, Addison-Wesley, 2004.

Kent Beck does an excellent job of introducing the motivation behind continuous integration, nightly builds, and prototypes. The Extreme Programming literature is in general filled with many useful ideas and practices.

[Hunt and Thomas 2000] Hunt, Andrew and Thomas, David, *The Pragmatic Programmer,* Addison Wesley, 2000.

This is an excellent book for software developers, and I highly recommend it. Some of the practices described in this book are derived from the pragmatic programmer.

Chapter 5: Defect Prevention

[Beck 2004] Beck, Kent, *Extreme Programming Explained,* 2nd Edition, Addison-Wesley, 2004.

> Extreme programming is the methodology that introduced test-driven development and pair programming. These practices are very well described in Kent Beck's book that introduced Extreme Programming.

Test-Driven Development

[Astels 2003] Astels, David, *Test Driven Development: A Practical Guide,* Prentice Hall PTR, 2003.

> I think this is one of the best books currently available on test-driven development. The author provides an excellent overview of different aspects of test-driven development. I especially like the chapters on the testing of user interfaces and mock objects.

[Beck 2002a] Beck, Kent, *Test Driven Development: By Example,* Addison-Wesley Professional, 2002.

[Husted and Massol 2003] Husted, Ted and Massol, Vincent, *JUnit in Action,* Manning Publications, 2003.

Automated Testing (General)

www.testing.com : I highly recommend this web site by Brian Marick. The page on *Classic Testing Mistakes* in particular is highly recommended.

[Marick 1995] Marick, Brian, *The Craft of Software Testing,* Prentice Hall, 1995.

Usability Testing

[Dumas and Redish 1999] Dumas, Joseph S. and Redish, Janice C., *A Practical Guide to Usability Testing,* Intellect, Ltd. (UK), 1999.

[Rubin 1994] Rubin, Jeffrey, *Handbook of Usability Testing: How to Plan, Design, and Conduct Effective Tests,* Wiley, 1994.

Other

[Ronsse et al 2003] Ronsse, Michiel, De Boschere, Koen, Christiaens, Mark, Chassin de Kergommeaux, Jacques, and Kranzmuller, Dieter, *Record / Replay for Nondeterministic Program Executions*, Communications of the ACM, September 2003 Volume 46, Number 9.

> This is an excellent paper that describes the issues in implementing a record and playback. The authors describe how i/o devices, message passing programs, and shared memory can be included in a record/playback architecture.

[Thomas and Hunt 2002] Thomas, Dave and Hunt, Andy, *Mock Objects*, IEEE Software, May/June 2002.

> This is a good introduction to mock objects. There are many good resources online too.

Chapter 6: Emphasis on Design

[Fowler: *Is Design Dead?*] Fowler, Martin, *Is Design Dead?*, http://www .martinfowler.com/articles/designDead.html.

> This is a web article that Martin Fowler continually updates. It is a must read for anyone who is interested in software design, especially in the context of agile development.

Design Patterns

[Gamma et al 1995] Gamma, Erich, Helm, Richard, Johnson, Ralph, and Vlissides, John, *Design Patterns,* Addison Wesley Professional, 1995.

> This is a software development classic and should be a standard reference for every software developer. There is also a great deal of knowledge available on the web about these and other patterns. I highly recommend a web search for the keywords *design patterns*.

[Fowler 2002] Fowler, Martin, *Patterns of Enterprise Architecture,* Addison-Wesley, 2002.

> Another useful book of design patterns for use with the web, databases, servers, etc.

Design Patterns, Agile Development, and Simple Design

[Evans 2003] Evans, Eric, *Domain-Driven Design,* Addison-Wesley, 2003.

> This is one of the best software design books in my opinion. It fits extremely well with agile development and an emphasis on simple design within a design vision as described in the *Emphasis on Design* chapter, though the terminology is different.

[Kerievsky 2004] Kerievsky, Joshua, *Refactoring to Patterns,* Addison-Wesley Professional, 2004.

> An excellent book that deals with the hard-core coding problems of balancing the up-front use of design patterns versus having them emerge over time through refactoring.

[Martin 2002] Martin, Robert C., *Agile Software Development, Principles, Patterns, and Practices,* Prentice Hall, 2002.

> This book is unfortunately misnamed. The value of this book is in understanding the drawbacks of various design patterns and in general how to employ design patterns in an agile development context. Highly recommended.

Refactoring

[Fowler 1999] Fowler, Martin, *Refactoring: Improving the Design of Existing Code,* Addison-Wesley, 1999.

> The bible of refactoring. Enough said!

Other

[Ambler and Jeffries 2002] Ambler, Scott W., Jeffries, Ron, *Agile Modeling,* Wiley, 2002.

> This book contains a rich description of some lightweight ideas for documenting designs.

[Armitage 2004] Armitage, John, *Are Agile Methods Good for Design?,* IEEE Transactions, Jan/Feb 2004.

> This is an excellent paper on user interface design for projects that employ agile development.

Chapter 7: Continual Refinement

[Cockburn 2004] Cockburn, Alistair, *Crystal Clear: A Human-Powered Methodology for Small Teams,* Addison-Wesley Professional, 2004.

> Alistair Cockburn provides useful and unique insights into the requirements of software development done by small teams.

[Cohn 2004] Cohn, Mike, *User Stories Applied: For Agile Software Development,* Addison-Wesley Professional, 2004.

> I highly recommend this book. It is packed with practical insights into how to gather requirements and write effective user stories for agile development.

[Cohn 2005] Cohn, Mike, *A Regular Heartbeat: The Benefits of Fixed Iteration Lengths*, 27 January 2005, Cutter Consortium Agile Project Management e-Mail Advisor, e-mail: apm@cutter.com.

> A short but useful article that describes the benefit of a regular heartbeat for projects.

[Crane 2002] Crane, Thomas G., *The Heart of Coaching,* FTA Press, 2002.

> This is one of my favorite books on coaching.

[Highsmith 2004a] Highsmith, Jim, *Agile Project Management,* 2004.

> This is **the** definitive work on agile project management and an excellent source book of ideas and insight into agile methods.

[Kerth 2001] Kerth, Norm, *Project Retrospectives: A Handbook for Team Reviews,* Dorset House, 2001.

> Although this book describes multi-day retrospectives that are usually held at the end of a project, there are many excellent ideas in the book that can be easily adapted for shorter, more agile-appropriate retrospectives. This is the reference you must have if you are interested in effective retrospectives.

[Larman 2003] Larman, Craig, *Agile and Iterative Development: A Manager's Guide,* Addison-Wesley Professional, 2003.

> The value of this book is that it is written for managers and executives to help them understand, support, and apply agile development. This is the only book that I'm aware of that directly discusses the business value of agile development, since business value is an important consideration for the target audience.

[Poppendieck and Poppendieck 2003] Poppendieck, Mary and Poppendieck, Tom, *Lean Software Development,* Addison-Wesley Professional, 2003.

> Lean development takes a unique approach to agile development: identifying the simplest set of practices possible that lead to effective software development. If you have heard of lean manufacturing, then this book will be of great interest because the thinking and rationale are similar.

[Schwaber and Beedle 2001] Schwaber, Ken and Beedle, Mike, *Agile Software Development with SCRUM,* Prentice Hall, 2001.

> SCRUM gets a lot of attention because it is a simple agile project management technique.

Chapter 8: Making Culture Change Happen

[Beck 2002b] Beck, Kent, *XP and Culture Change*, Cutter IT Journal, Cutter Consortium, Oct 2002.

> Kent Beck discusses culture change required for Extreme Programming from the standpoint of the various stakeholders, especially developers and managers. You should be able to get a copy of this publication from www.cutter.com.

[Cockburn 2001] Cockburn, Alistair, *Agile Software Development,* Addison-Wesley, 2001.

> Many factors with the physical work environment and the impact it can have on agile development are described in this book.

[Crane 2002] Crane, Thomas G., *The Heart of Coaching,* FTA Press, 2002.

> This is one of my favorite books on coaching. There is a very useful chapter on culture change and the role that individual and team coaching plays in achieving culture change.

[Kotter 1996] Kotter, John P., *Leading Change,* Harvard Business School Press, 1996.

> This book describes the problems that are commonly faced when attempting culture change in an organization. The value of the book is in the strategy that is outlined for achieving change.

[Lindval et al 2004] Mikael Lindval, Dirk Muthig, Aldo Dagnino, Christina Wallin, Michael Stupperich, David Kiefer, John May, and Tuomo Kahkonen, *Agile Software Development in Large Organizations,* IEEE Computer, December 2004.

> The authors of this paper outline a number of good points related to attempting to introduce agile development into large organizations such as Motorola, Nokia, and DaimlerChrysler.

Conclusion

I believe today (because I am always learning and adapting) that the principles outlined in this book are key ingredients to attaining sustainability. At the very least, teams who are willing to take on the challenge of sustainability will have an excellent headstart on their journey by adopting the mindset outlined and carefully considering and adopting each of the practices with a goal toward continual improvement.

I have tried to develop and follow a few key themes in this book:

- Software development is a complex undertaking. The software industry needs to mature, but in order to do so, we need to match the development methods we use with the complexity of the software technology ecosystem, which forces the need for continual change.
- The methods that are still predominantly taught in school and employed in industry are *code-then-fix,* or the waterfall method. These methods are inadequate to the task because they are change-adverse and are either too lax (*code-then-fix*) or impose too much ceremony and process (waterfall).
- The principles and practices employed in this book are directly from agile development. Agile methods are intended to provide *just enough* ceremony and process to allow teams to get their job done in a lightweight manner. Unfortunately, some people associate agile development with being not disciplined when in fact agile development requires a great deal of discipline, as should be obvious when reading this and other agile books.
- Agile development requires specific project management practices *and* an emphasis on technical excellence *and* collaboration. It is too easy to apply agile project management practices such as iterative development and forget that the state of the software being worked

on (e.g., maintainability, design and architecture, etc.) and whether the development team includes users (and/or user representatives) and business people that collaborate on the project also greatly influences agility.

- Although my background is one where my focus is on producing shrink-wrapped software products, a *product* could be any kind of software: a web site, IT system such as a database backend, firmware, consulting project, etc.

- Too many projects can't cope with the complexity of the software development undertaking. The result is *unsustainable development*, where teams are largely only able to *respond* to changes in their ecosystem. They have little control and are almost always in catch-up mode. The most effort goes toward adding features and fixing bugs. These projects respond to complexity with complex solutions that are unreliable (i.e., buggy), brittle (break easily), and unable to support future change.

- In *sustainable development*, teams are able to be *proactive* about changes in their ecosystem. Their ability to be proactive is enabled by their attention to doing the work that is of the highest value to customers with high quality and reliability and an eye toward continual improvement *despite* increasing complexity.

- Sustainable development requires acknowledging the need for change. This means adopting a different mindset and being uncompromising in four key areas: a working product every day, continual refinement, defect prevention over detection, and an emphasis on lightweight but continual design. *Sustainable development* results, where it is possible to be proactive about change.

- The first principle of sustainable development is *having a working product every day*. A working product, even if it is not functionally complete, gives teams flexibility and allows them to be much more responsive to changes in their ecosystem (user requirements, competitive threats, sales opportunities, etc.) and proactive when opportunities arise. This flexibility is crucial in sustainability.

- The second principle of sustainable development is *defect prevention*. Defect prevention is a change in mindset for virtually all teams, where instead of using the *code-then-fix* mentality to development, the team does everything in its power to prevent defects reaching customers.

Central to defect prevention is the practice of ruthless testing, where computers are relied upon to do the repetitive and boring testing tasks that people do today. This allows people to concentrate on the more creative aspects of testing, such as testing organizations using the product in realistic ways as the product is developed.

- The third principle of sustainable development is *design emphasis.* Design matters, and good design is required to ensure that the product is designed to promote future maintainability and modifiability, both of which are crucial elements in sustainable development. Teams also need to understand how to design what they are working on. Simple design, refactoring, and design patterns all play important roles in design. Every project and team has to find the right balance between iterative design and up-front design. When they do up-front design, however, it is not done in the traditional way that is heavy on documentation, but rather through lightweight collaborative design sessions and the use of design patterns. Design experience and domain expertise is vital in ensuring that teams do not rely on up-front design and design patterns too much because there should always be a bias toward iterative design.

- The final principle of sustainable development is *continual refinement.* Continual refinement applies to how the project is planned and tracked through iterative development. Equally important is that continual refinement is required for *how* the project is approached, so that the team can continually enhance its development processes and collaboration.

- The discipline of iterative development is still useful in applications where continual change is not necessary, possible, or desired. These are projects such as software used in medical analysis (where people can get hurt if there is a defect) or projects with set milestones that must be met in a certain order. This is because even if there is little change in the iteration plans, the simple discipline of being able to plan and track progress is highly valuable.

- Because culture change is most often required to achieve the necessary mindset, I have included a chapter as a starter toward achieving the change.

I hope you, the reader, find this book useful.

References

[Ambler and Jeffries 2002] Ambler, Scott W., Jeffries, Ron, *Agile Modeling,* Wiley, 2002. See also www.agilemodeling.com and www.agiledata.org.

[Armitage 2004] Armitage, John, *Are Agile Methods Good for Design?*, IEEE Transactions, Jan/Feb 2004.

[Astels 2003] Astels, David, *Test Driven Development: A Practical Guide,* Prentice Hall PTR, 2003.

[Auer and Miller 2001] Auer, Ken, and Miller, Roy, *Extreme Programming Applied,* Addison-Wesley Professional, 2001.

[Bandaru 2004] Bandaru, V., *Understanding XP: A CMM Perspecitive*, DeveloperIQ, Oct 2004.

[Beck 2002a] Beck, Kent, *Test Driven Development: By Example,* Addison-Wesley Professional, 2002.

[Beck 2002b] Beck, Kent, *XP and Culture Change*, Cutter IT Journal, Cutter Consortium, Oct 2002.

[Beck 2004] Beck, Kent, *Extreme Programming Explained,* 2nd Edition, Addison-Wesley, 2004.

[Boehm and Turner 2004] Boehm, Barry, and Turner, Richard, *Balancing Agility and Discipline,* Addison-Wesley, 2004.

[Buckingham and Coffman 1999] Buckingham, Marcus, and Coffman, Curt, *First, Break All the Rules,* Simon & Schuster, 1999.

[Christensen 2003] Clayton M. Christensen, *The Innovator's Dilemma,* HarperBusiness, 2003.

[Christensen and Raynor 2003] Christensen, Clayton M., and Raynor, Michael E., *The Innovator's Solution,* Harvard Business School Press, 2003.

[Cockburn 2001] Cockburn, Alistair, *Agile Software Development,* Addison-Wesley, 2001.

[Cockburn 2004] Cockburn, Alistair, *Crystal Clear: A Human-Powered Methodology for Small Teams,* Addison-Wesley Professional, 2004.

[Cohn 2004] Cohn, Mike, *User Stories Applied: For Agile Software Development,* Addison-Wesley Professional, 2004.

[Cohn 2005] Cohn, Mike, *A Regular Heartbeat: The Benefits of Fixed Iteration Lengths*, 27 January 2005, Cutter Consortium Agile Project Management e-Mail Advisor, e-mail: apm@cutter.com.

[Collins 2001] Collins, Jim, *Good to Great,* HarperBusiness, 2001.

[Collins and Porras 2002] Collins, Jim, and Porras, Jerry I., *Built to Last: Successful Habits of Visionary Companies,* HarperBusiness, 2002.

[Cox 1986] Cox, B.J., *Object-Oriented Programming: An Evolutionary Approach,* Addison-Wesley, 1986.

[Crane 2002] Crane, Thomas G., *The Heart of Coaching,* FTA Press, 2002.

[Demarco and Lister 1999] Demarco, Tom, and Lister, Timothy, *Peopleware: Productive Projects and Teams,* 2nd Edition, Dorset House, 1999.

[Dumas and Redish 1999] Dumas, Joseph S., and Redish, Janice C., *A Practical Guide to Usability Testing,* Intellect, Ltd. (UK), 1999.

[Economist 2004] *Make it Simple: A Survey of Information Technology*, The Economist, October 2004.

[Evans 2003] Evans, Eric, *Domain-Driven Design,* Addison-Wesley, 2003.

[Fowler 1999] Fowler, Martin, *Refactoring: Improving the Design of Existing Code,* Addison-Wesley, 1999.

[Fowler: *Is Design Dead?*] Fowler, Martin, *Is Design Dead?*, http://www.martinfowler.com/articles/designDead.html.

[Fowler 2002] Fowler, Martin, *Patterns of Enterprise Architecture,* Addison-Wesley, 2002.

[Gamma et al 1995] Gamma, Erich, Helm, Richard, Johnson, Ralph, and Vlissides, John, *Design Patterns,* Addison-Wesley Professional, 1995.

[Glazer 2001] Glazer, Hillel, *Dispelling the Process Myth: Having a Process Does Not Mean Sacrificing Agility or Creativity*, Crosstalk: The Journal of Defense Software Engineering, November 2001.

[Grady 1997] Grady, Robert B., *Successful Software Process Improvement,* Prentice Hall PTR, 1997.

[Highsmith 1999] Highsmith, Jim, *Adaptive Software Development: A Collaborative Approach to Managing Complex Systems,* Dorset House, 1999.

[Highsmith 2002] Highsmith, Jim, *Agile Development Ecosystems,* Addison-Wesley, 2002.

[Highsmith 2004a] Highsmith, Jim, *Agile Project Management,* 2004.

[Highsmith 2004b] Highsmith, Jim, *Planning and Scanning,* 9 December 2004, Cutter Consortium Agile Project Management e-Mail Advisor, e-mail: apm@cutter.com.

[Highsmith 2005] Highsmith, Jim, *The Limits of Evolutionary Design*, 6 January 2005, Cutter Consortium Agile Project Management e-Mail Advisor, e-mail: apm@cutter.com.

[Hohmann 1996] Hohmann, Luke, *The Journey of the Software Professional: The Sociology of Software Development,* Prentice Hall PTR, 1996.

[Hunt and Thomas 2000] Hunt, Andrew, and Thomas, David, *The Pragmatic Programmer,* Addison-Wesley, 2000.

[Husted and Massol 2003] Husted, Ted, and Massol, Vincent, *JUnit in Action,* Manning Publications, 2003.

[Jeffries et al 2000] Jeffries, Ron, Ann Anderson, Chet Hendrickson, and Ronald E. Jeffries, *Extreme Programming Installed,* Addison-Wesley Professional, 2000.

[Kerievsky 2004] Kerievsky, Joshua, *Refactoring to Patterns,* Addison-Wesley Professional, 2004.

[Kerth 2001] Kerth, Norm, *Project Retrospectives: A Handbook for Team Reviews,* Dorset House, 2001.

[Kotter 1996] Kotter, John P., *Leading Change,* Harvard Business School Press, 1996.

[Larman 2003] Larman, Craig, *Agile and Iterative Development: A Manager's Guide,* Addison-Wesley Professional, 2003.

[Lindval et al 2004] Lindvall, Mikael, Muthig, Dirk, Dagnino, Aldo, Wallin, Christina, Stupperich, Michael, Kiefer, David, May, John, and Kahkonen, Tuomo, *Agile Software Development in Large Organizations,* IEEE Computer, December 2004.

[Link and Frolich 2003] Link, Johannes, and Frolich, Peter, *Unit Testing in Java,* Morgan Kaufmann, 2003.

[Lundin et al 2000] Lundin, Stephen C., Paul, Harry, and Christensen, John, *Fish! A Remarkable Way to Improve Morale and Boost Results,* Hyperion, 2000.

[Lynn and Reilly 2002] Lynn, Gary S., and Reilly, Richard P., *Blockbusters: The Five Keys to Developing GREAT New Products,* HarperBusiness, 2002.

[Marick 1995] Marick, Brian, *The Craft of Software Testing,* Prentice-Hall, 1995. See also www.testing.com.

[Martin 2002] Martin, Robert C., *Agile Software Development, Principles, Patterns, and Practices,* Prentice Hall, 2002.

[McConnell 1996] McConnell, Steve, *Rapid Development,* Microsoft Press, 1996.

[McGrenere 2000] McGrenere, Joanna, *Bloat: The Objective and Subjective Dimensions*, Department of Computer Science, University of Toronto, CHI 2000.

[Moore 2002] Moore, Geoffrey A., *Crossing the Chasm: Marketing and Selling Disruptive Products to Mainstream Customers,* HarperBusiness, 2002.

[Norman 1999] Norman, Donald A., *The Invisible Computer,* MIT Press, 1999.

[Palmer and Felsing 2002] Palmer, Stephen R. and Felsing, John M., *A Practical Guide to Feature-Driven Development,* Prentice Hall PTR, 2002.

[Paulk et al 1993] Paulk, M.C., Curtis, B., Chrissis, M.B., and Weber, C.V., *Capability Maturity Model, Version 1.1*, *IEEE Software*, Vol. 10 No. 4 (July 1993), pp. 18–27.

[Paulk 2001] Paulk, Mark C., *Extreme Programming from a CMM Perspective*, XP Universe, July 2001.

[Poppendieck and Poppendieck 2003] Poppendieck, Mary, and Poppendieck, Tom, *Lean Software Development,* Addison-Wesley Professional, 2003.

[Pressman 1992] Pressman, Roger S., *Software Engineering, A Practitioner's Approach,* 3rd Edition, McGraw Hill, New York, 1992.

[Repenning and Sterman 2001] Repenning, Nelson P., and Sterman, John D., *Nobody Ever Gets Credit for Fixing Problems That Never Happened: Creating and Sustaining Process Improvement*, California Management Review, Vol. 43 No. 4, Summer 2001.

[Ronsse et al 2003] Ronsse, Michiel, De Boschere, Koen, Christiaens, Mark, Chassin de Kergommeaux, Jacques, and Kranzmuller, Dieter, *Record/Replay for Nondeterministic Program Executions*, Communications of the ACM, September 2003 Volume 46, Number 9.

[Rothman 2000] Rothman, Johanna, *What Does It Cost You to Fix a Defect? And Why Should You Care?*, www.catapulse.com, October 2000.

[Rubin 1994] Rubin, Jeffrey, *Handbook of Usability Testing: How to Plan, Design, and Conduct Effective Tests,* Wiley, 1994.

[Schwaber and Beedle 2001] Schwaber, Ken, and Beedle, Mike, *Agile Software Development with SCRUM,* Prentice Hall, 2001.

[Stapleton 2003] Stapleton, Jennifer, *DSDM: Business Focused Development,* Pearson Education, 2003. See also www.dsdm.org.

[Thomas and Hunt 2002] Thomas, Dave, and Hunt, Andy, *Mock Objects*, IEEE Software, May/June 2002.

[Thornton 1996] Thornton, Ian, *Krakatau: The Destruction and Reassembly of an Island Ecosystem,* Harvard University Press, 1996.

[Womack and Jones 1996] Womack, James P., and Jones, Daniel T., *Lean Thinking: Banish Waste and Create Wealth in Your Corporation,* Simon and Schuster, 1996.

Index

no broken windows practice
and, 49
practices for preventing, 179
pragmatic practices for, 52
preventing, 73, 212
preventing from reaching
customers, 42
preventing vs. detecting, 31,
33, 73
prioritizing, 101
programming and code reviews
and, 98
quality assurance and, 73, 76
rearchitecture and, 123
root-cause analysis and, 100
ruthless testing for, 78
time spent fixing, 13
tools for, 92
tracking, 52
uncompromising attitude
towards, 50
won't fix, 101
working product and, 42
Dell Computers, 19
design, 107, 213
bottom-up, 108
discussions, 122
emphasis on, 33
extreme, 108
Extreme Programming and, 192
for reuse, 128
for testability, 84
frequent meetings in, 122
guiding principles in, 112–113
patterns in, 119
practices for, 180
rearchitecture and, 123
refactoring and, 117
reviews, 122
simplicity in, 115
top-down, 108

vision in, 112
deterministic programs, 85
discipline, 36, 142
Extreme Programming and, 193
disruptive technologies, 18
diversity, 153
documentation
barely sufficient, 53
code reviews and, 100
dangers of excessive, 55
design and, 110
in plan-driven development, 22
source code, 95
updating, 44
doxygen, 55
dynamic systems development
method (DSDM), 194

Eclipse, 45
education, 154, 211
emergent design, 108. *See also*
design, 195
engineering approach to software
development, 27
engineering, guiding principles
for, 112–113
errors, defect prevention and, 93
Eve, 114
event logging, 95
evolutionary design, 108. *See also*
design, 195
exception handling, 93
execution profilers, 94
exit criteria, 53
expertise, 22
external dependencies, 18
Extreme Programming
design in, 192
misconceptions of, 192
practices for, 184
strengths of, 185

Register
Your Book

at www.awprofessional.com/register

You may be eligible to receive:

- Advance notice of forthcoming editions of the book
- Related book recommendations
- Chapter excerpts and supplements of forthcoming titles
- Information about special contests and promotions throughout the year
- Notices and reminders about author appearances, tradeshows, and online chats with special guests

Contact us

If you are interested in writing a book or reviewing manuscripts prior to publication, please write to us at:

Editorial Department
Addison-Wesley Professional
75 Arlington Street, Suite 300
Boston, MA 02116 USA
Email: AWPro@aw.com

Visit us on the Web: http://www.awprofessional.com

Instill Collaboration in Your Projects with *Collaboration Explained: Facilitation Skills for Collaborative Leaders*

by Jean Tabaka
0-321-26877-6

Designed for XP coaches, Scrum Masters, Crystal Clear practitioners, and all agile project managers, *Collaboration Explained* reviews the fundamentals of collaboration:

- Primary collaboration roles and events
- Collaboration techniques
- What to do for distributed, virtual teams
- Guidelines for conducting key collaboration activities in your projects

Jean Tabaka has an extensive background as a programmer, project manager, and most recently methodologist, specializing in agile and adaptive software development environments for internal IT departments, ISVs, and consulting organizations. She has created and implemented both rigorous and agile methodologies for Qwest Communications, Siebel Systems, Sybase, Inc., and several smaller firms. She is currently the lead Agile Mentor at Rally Software Development, guiding customers in adopting agile principles and practices and has been working in and writing about collaborative approaches in software projects for more than four years.

With this book, Tabaka presents the collaboration techniques she has developed as "how-to" steps and applies them across a variety of agile methodologies focusing on the application of practices for agile teams, customers, and testers.

Straightforward, practical, and simple, *Collaboration Explained* cuts through the fluff and gives you what you need to effectively put collaboration into practice.

For more information on this title please visit www.awprofessional.com/title/0321268776.

informIT

www.informit.com

YOUR GUIDE TO IT REFERENCE

Articles

Keep your edge with thousands of free articles, in-depth features, interviews, and IT reference recommendations — all written by experts you know and trust.

Online Books

Answers in an instant from **InformIT Online Book's** 600+ fully searchable on line books. For a limited time, you can get your first 14 days **free**.

Safari
TECH BOOKS ONLINE

Catalog

Review online sample chapters, author biographies and customer rankings and choose exactly the right book from a selection of over 5,000 titles.

Wouldn't it be great

if the world's leading technical publishers joined forces to deliver their best tech books in a common digital reference platform?

They have. Introducing
InformIT Online Books
powered by Safari.

■ **Specific answers to specific questions.**

InformIT Online Books' powerful search engine gives you relevance-ranked results in a matter of seconds.

■ **Immediate results.**

With InformIT Online Books, you can select the book you want and view the chapter or section you need immediately.

■ **Cut, paste and annotate.**

Paste code to save time and eliminate typographical errors. Make notes on the material you find useful and choose whether or not to share them with your work group.

■ **Customized for your enterprise.**

Customize a library for you, your department or your entire organization. You only pay for what you need.

Get your first 14 days FREE!

For a limited time, InformIT Online Books is offering its members a 10 book subscription risk-free for 14 days. Visit **http://www.informit.com/onlinebooks** for details.